JUSTICE LOUIS D. BRANDEIS
The Zionist Chapter of His Life

JUSTICE LOUIS D. BRANDEIS

The Zionist Chapter of His Life

by Ezekiel Rabinowitz

Philosophical Library

New York

Dedicated to my wife, my daughter
and grandchildren, Sheera and Adam.

ACKNOWLEDGMENTS

I wish to express my heartiest thanks and profound appreciation for the valuable assistance given me by:
Mrs. Sylvia Landress, Director of the Zionist Archives and Library in New York and her assistants, Mrs. Rachel Schechtman and Miss Esther Togman; Miss Judith A. Schiff, Librarian, Historical Manuscripts and University Archives, Yale University; Harry Alderman, Librarian, American Jewish Committee, Blaustein Library; Aaron Baroway and Miss Dubby Goldberg.

CONTENTS

Chapter 1

THE ZIONIST MOVEMENT IN THE UNITED STATES
BEFORE BRANDEIS

In 1896 newspaper articles from abroad revealed the appearance of a book called *Der Judenstaat* by Dr. Theodor Herzl who proclaimed the rebirth of the Jewish nation. When Herzl issued his call for the first Zionist Congress, Chicago was the first city to respond, as the result of the formation in 1895 of the Chicago Zionist Society, which later became the "Knights of Zion." The Knights of Zion was chartered in 1896, and it was Leon Zolotkoff, noted Jewish journalist, who represented this group as the delegate to the First Zionist World Congress. It anticipated its Eastern sister by more than a year.

Steps were taken after the first Zionist Congress to bring together the scattered Zionist societies in New York and several other cities, and a convention held in New York in 1898 resulted in the formation of the Federation of American Zionists with Professor Richard Gottheil as President and Rabbi Stephen S. Wise as Secretary. Both of these personalities were adherents of Herzl's political Zionism. Zionist activities at the time consisted mainly of propaganda which was quite successful among the Jewish immigrants from Russia, Austria and Rumania. The opposition to Zionism, mainly from West European Jews, declared Zionism as a travesty of patriotism.

Among the resolutions at the Third Annual Convention of the Federation of American Zionists in June, 1900, was one recommending that "the delegates to the Zionist Congress are to endeavor to induce Dr. Herzl to visit America and thus strengthen the movement in this country." [1]

1. *American Jewish Year Book 5662*

In his *Diaries*, dated May 23, 1897, Dr. Herzl writes as follows:

"The movement is beginning in America.

"Michael Singer, editor of the new weekly, *Toleranz*, sends me reports about meetings in New York, etc.

"A conference of rabbies, with Dr. Gottheil as its head, has come out in favor of our movement.

"On May 10 the *New York Sun* published articles about Zionism.

"When I showed the *Sun* column to Benedikt yesterday, he said benevolently: 'You are driving the whole world crazy. A real Pied Piper of Hamelin'." [2]

In his diary of the same date he writes:

". . . Haas writes that people in America want me to make a 'lecture tour' on the other side." [3]

Herzl at that time was too busy to make a trip to the United States. The East European masses responded to his Zionist ideas and the Zionist organization grew everywhere, especially in Russia.

According to the report of the Honorary Secretary of the Actions Comité, Oscar Marmoreck, at the Fifth International Zionist Congress in Basel, in 1901, Zionism is growing stronger in various countries:

"In Germany the number of Zionists has doubled. The number of delegates present was 278. Of greatest interest were the sectional meetings of the Russian delegates and visitors, representing an aggregate of 965 associations in Russia, extending from Kovno to Tchita on the Manchurian frontier, and from St. Petersburg to Astrakhan on the Caspian Sea." [4]

The roots of Russian Zionism date back to the early eighteen eighties when the Chovevei Zion (the Lovers of Zion) formulated a Palestine Program, the aim of which was to make Palestine a Jewish Spiritual Center. Achad Ha'am, the most respected representative of modern Hebrew literature, was one of its most prominent leaders, and the movement was often referred to as

2. *The Complete Diaries of Theodor Herzl, Vol. II* (p. 552)
3. Ibid. (p. 553)
4. *American Jewish Year Book 5663*

Achad-Haamism. It was cultural not political Zionism. The significant growth of the movement, however, came after Herzl's political Zionism was proclaimed at the First Zionist Congress in 1897. Zionism in Russia was officially declared illegal, with the exception of about eight months during the Kerensky Revolution in 1917. This hostility was renewed when the Bolshevik Party seized control.

Just a few illustrations about the circumstances under which Zionists had to carry on their work:

In March 1908, the Czar pardoned all participants in the pogroms of 1905.[5]

October 2, 1909: Orders received from St. Petersburg by the Governor of Kiev forbade all Zionist activities.[6]

April 8, 1910: Dr. J. B. Sapir, member of the Zionist Actions Comité ,was arrested in Odessa for making collections for the National Fund.[7]

July 22, 1910: The Governor of Poltava refused to confirm the election of Mr. Friedenberg as Crown Rabbi of Kremenchug, on the ground that he participated in the Zionist Congress.[8]

July 22, 1910: Zionist National Fund boxes were confiscated by the police in Opto (Radom).[9]

August 26, 1910: Former Crown Rabbi of Odessa, Dr. Avinovitzky, compelled, in spite of illness, to serve a sentence of imprisonment for two weeks for keeping a collection box of the Zionist National Fund.[10]

September 16, 1910: Issuance of cheap pilgrimage passports (costing half a rouble) to Palestine, prohibited to Jews.[11]

September 12, 1913: At Odessa, Prefect dismissed wardens of local synagogues for allowing Zionist propaganda there. Advocate Greenbaum, Russian delegate, arrested at frontier on return from Zionist Congress.[13]

5. *American Jewish Year Book* 5668
6. *American Jewish Year Book* 5671
7. Ibid.
8. Ibid.
9. *American Jewish Year Book* 5672
10. Ibid.
11. Ibid.
13. *American Jewish Year Book* 5675

October 14, 1913: At Odessa, steamer leaving for Palestine stopped because Jewish emigrants sang *Hatikvah;* leader arrested and foreign passport canceled.[14]

In spite of all these persecutions, Zionism in Russia grew. At the Seventh Zionist Congress in 1905, for instance, among the close to six hundred delegates present, four hundred came from Russia.[15]

Since Herzl could not at that time accept the invitation for a propaganda tour in the United States, he persuaded Jacob de Haas to undertake the trip. De Haas was Herzl's secretary in English in 1897 and at four Zionist Congresses. He was one of the conveners of the First Zionist Congress. He came to the United States in 1902, became secretary of the Federation of American Zionists and editor of the *Maccabean,* its official publication. He later moved to Boston where he edited *The Jewish Advocate.*

At the 16th Annual Convention of the Federation of American Zionists, held in Cincinnati, Ohio, in June 1913, De Haas wanted to know why there were only 500 organized Zionists in New York.[16]

At the 15th Annual Convention of the Federation, held in Cleveland, in June 1912, Louis Lipsky, Chairman of the Executive Committee, had given a very clear answer to this question:

". . . A large plan of Zionist propaganda is impossible under the conditions that hem us in. A large plan, a movement that would impress and strike the entire Jewish community, is impossible without a large corps of energetic workers, backed by a capital fund of ample proportions to make the expenditure of energy worthwhile.

"This capital fund we have not. The large corps of energetic workers we have not. What we do possess is a small band of enthusiastic men and women who believe we make the best of. What we have done this year, little as it seems to be, has been possible because of the existence of this small group, each bring-

14. Ibid.
15. Ibid.
16. *Maccabean,* July 1913

4

ing his mite of self-sacrifice. Zionism is as yet no mass movement." [17]

The low ebb of the Zionist movement in the United States was in 1914 confronted with the war in Europe which brought a crisis upon the Zionist World Organization. The members of the Actions Comité [18] were scattered. The Central Bureau in Berlin was crippled. The Federations of England, Germany and Austria were partially or wholly disabled. Palestine, which was hitherto aided in the most ample measure by the Jews of these countries, and especially Russia, was now bereft of their support. The achievements of a generation were imperiled.

The appearance at this critical period of the attorney Louis Dembitz Brandeis was a real miracle.

17. *Maccabean,* July 1912
18. Action Comité is the world Zionist Executive Committee

Chapter 2

THE FIGHT OF THE ANTI-ZIONISTS AGAINST
"DUAL ALLEGIANCE"

In 1914, when Louis D. Brandeis took over the Zionist leadership there were about three million Jews in the United States but no more than twelve thousand enrolled members in the Federation of American Zionists. The main reason why the opposition to Zionism was so successful was their propaganda argument that Zionism is a sin against patriotism. The Jewish Fraternal Orders, for instance, in their hearts in full sympathy with the Zionist aspirations, were indifferent mainly because of fear of being accused of lack of patriotism.

When Brandeis, known throughout the country as the "People's Attorney," entered the scene, the Zionist movement did find its second Herzl. His statements:

"There is no inconsistency between loyalty to America and loyalty to the Jewish spirit";

"Let no American imagine that Zionism is inconsistent with patriotism";

"Loyalty to America demands that each Jew become a Zionist"; were like the explosion of a bombshell against the anti-Zionists. The accusation of dual allegiance became untenable and absurd. It gave a chance to many "non-Zionists" to get up and say so.

During May and June 1915, for instance, "the two great Orders, the Independent Order Brith Abraham and the Independent Order Brith Shalom declared themselves Zionistic, and pledged themselves to give moral and financial support to the

Zionist movement. This meant more than 100,000 possible Zionists." [1]

At that time, many years before, and many years later, Reform Judaism remained true to the principles advocated by their leader Isaac Mayer Wise that Judaism is separated from nationalism.

"At the founding in 1841, of America's first Reform Temple, Gustav Posnansky uttered a momentous slogan which was to become the rallying point of powerful forces opposed to Zionism: 'This country is our Palestine, this city is our Jerusalem, this house of God, our Temple.' " [2]

At the 22nd Convention of the Union of American Hebrew Congregations on January 17, 1911, Rev. Dr. Kaufman Kohler, President of the Hebrew Union College, put it this way:

". . . For the Union the opportunity came somewhat later to place itself on record to advocate the Reform principle, when, in 1898, in view of the Zionist movement, it declared itself to be unalterably opposed to political Zionism, and America to be the home and the Zion of hope of the American Jew, Judaism's mission being spiritual, not political." [3]

The same spirit was in full swing among many other sections of the Jewish population:

At a conference held in New York on February 3rd and 4th, 1906, on the desirability of forming a representative body of the Jews which led to the formation of the American Jewish Committee, Mr. Louis Marshall during the discussion expressed his opinion "that the basis on which a representative body could be formed that was really American in character would be that of the Jewish Congregations of America as a unit. The method would be democratic, would recognize the Jews as a religious body, whereas any other method would be aristocratic and would recognize the Jews from the standpoint of race, which is inconsistent with American conception of government." [4]

1. *Maccabean,* June 1915
2. *The Political World of American Zionism,* Samuel Halperin (p. 71)
3. *Union of American Hebrew Congregations,* March 1911 (p. 6548)
4. *American Jewish Committee—Protocol of Meetings,* Vol. I

"On April 30, 1907, the resignation of Max L. Margulies, Professor of Biblical Exegesis at the Hebrew Union College, was accepted by the Board of Governors of the institution, the third professor to resign, the others being Henry Malter, Professor of Jewish Philosophy, and Max Schloessinger, Instructor in Jewish History and Literature. The resignations are variously designated as forced, on account of the Zionist partisanship of the professors." [5]

Hebrew Union College excludes Zionist Lecturer

One of the student organizations of the Hebrew Union College of Cincinnati invited Dr. Horace M. Kallen of Madison, Wisconsin, to lecture on "The Meaning of Hebraism."

But a few days before the lecture was scheduled to take place, he was notified by the president of the organization that "the Hebrew Union College authorities had demanded that the lecture be cancelled. The main reason was because Kallen was a Zionist." [6]

"Speaking in Kansas City, last month, before the Federation of Jewish Charities, Mr. Jacob H. Shiff finished his speech with the following appeal: 'Do not permit Zionism from over the seas to come among you.' " [7]

The question whether to issue a favorable statement on the Balfour Declaration was heatedly debated at the meetings of the Executive Committee of the American Jewish Committee. At the meeting on February 2, 1918, Mr. Marshall presented the following news report of a statement made by Professor Albert Bushnell Hart of Harvard University. In this statement published in the *Worcester Telegram*, Professor Hart declared that Jews either have to renounce their citizenship or else give up Zionism.

"The Jewish people must either fish or cut bait," he said. "They must either reject their American citizenship or renounce any such dangerous doctrine as Zionism.

". . . As long as this country will not release the Jews from

5. *American Jewish Year Book* 5668
6. *Maccabean*, January 1915
7. *Maccabean*, March 1915 (On Jan. 16, 1920, in the columns of the official Zionist organ, Shiff appealed to American Jewry to unite for the upbuilding of Palestine.)

8

citizenship and as long as the Jews themselves will not give up their citizenship, there can be no justification for dual allegiance.

"Zionism is a dangerous doctrine, and it is bound to be given up sooner or later by the Jewish people."

The President then presented the following communications from absent members. One of them, J. W. Bernheim, wrote:

"I regret my inability to be present at the meeting of the Executive Committee. The importance of the subject to be considered induced me to make the following brief statement defining my position.

"The indefinite expression in regard to Palestine by the British government was promptly seized by the Zionists in our country to create the impression that all American Israelites are ready to welcome the chance of rehabilitating that country and to create there a Jewish State. Our co-religionists of the Reform Church are fully aware of the danger which such an act is calculated to create in the public mind.

". . . I must respectfully urge that the Executive Committee keep to the middle of the road, abstaining from endorsing or supporting a movement fraught with the gravest consequences to American Israel."

Mr. Shiff said: "I believe if we should do one thing in the American Jewish Committee—you know how much nearer I have myself come to Zionism—but I believe if we would do one thing in the American Jewish Committee, we should not deal with this question, for if we do as a Committee, it is not at all unlikely that it will result in the breaking up of this Committee." [8]

The former Anti-Zionists, now classified as Non-Zionists, issued on behalf of the American Jewish Committee, a more or less favorable statement on the Balfour Declaration. The Anti-Zionists, however, regarding the situation as more dangerous than before, declared a real war:

Rabbi Julian H. Miller from Chattanooga appealed to President Wilson:

"Please do not take America from me . . . My flag is Red,

8. *American Jewish Committee—Protocol of Meetings*, Vol. IV

9

White and Blue, how then can I have any other National Homeland?" [9]

On March 24, 1919, Jacob De Haas, then in London, received a cable from New York informing him that ". . . Landman, Editor *American Hebrew*, sailed to Paris yesterday for anti-Zionist publicity campaign." [10]

Before the Peace Conference concluded its sessions, 299 Jews signed a "Statement to the Peace Conference" in which they rejected the idea for a Jewish Palestine for the present and the future.

On March 4, 1919, Congressman Julius Kahn of California, on behalf of a committee of 39 prominent Jews, presented a petition to President Wilson protesting against the establishment of a Jewish State in Palestine. The petitioners expressed "entire sympathy with the efforts of the Zionists, which claim to secure for Jews at present living in lands of oppression a refuge in Palestine or elsewhere, where they may freely develop their capabilities and carry on their activities as free citizens." But they "raise their voices in warning and protest against the demands of the Zionists for the reorganization of the Jews as a national unit, to whom now or in the future, territorial sovereignty shall be committed." [11]

Of this statement Ambassador Henry Morgenthau was one of the signers, and he, together with Congressman Julius Kahn, was asked to present these views to the Conference. In an article published in *The World's Work*, in July 1921, Morgenthau expressed his opinion as follows:

". . . Against such a political segregation of the Jews in Palestine, or elsewhere, we object, because the Jews are dedicated heart and soul to the welfare of the countries in which they dwell under free conditions. All Jews repudiate every suspicion of a double allegiance, but to our minds it is necessarily implied in and cannot by any logic be eliminated from establishment of a sovereign State for the Jews in Palestine." [12]

9. *The Palestine Question in the Wilson Era*, Selig Adler (p. 312)
10. *De Hass Papers*, Reel 5 (Zionist Archives and Library)
11. *American Jewish Year Book 5680*
12. *All In A Life Time*, Henry Morgenthau (pp. 349-50)

". . . Zionism is the most stupendous fallacy in Jewish history. I assert that it is wrong in principle and impossible of realization; that it is unsound in its economics, fantastic in its politics, and sterile in its spiritual ideals. Where it is not pathetically visionary, it is cruel, playing with the hopes of a people blindly seeking their way out of agelong miseries." [13]

That the Non-Zionists, who issued on behalf of the American Jewish Committee a favorable statement on the Balfour Declaration were still tortured by the fear of being accused of dual allegiance, can be seen from a letter by Marshall, dated July 12, 1918, to Major Lionel de Rothschild, President of the League of British Jews:

". . . We deemed it our duty," Marshall writes, "for many reasons, both practical and sentimental, to give expression to our attitude toward the Balfour Declaration, but at the same time considered it highly important to give emphasis to those controlling principles which we look upon as essential to the preservation of our status as American citizens."

". . . I may add that before our Committee adopted its Statement, I submitted the draft to Mr. Lansing, our Secretary of State, for his criticism and comments, and received his approval." [14]

Alas! The then Secretary of State, Robert Lansing, must have joined the Non-Zionists; up to that time he was a very devoted Anti-Zionist:

The Secretary of State to President Wilson
Washington, December 13, 1917

My dear Mr. President:
    There is being brought considerable pressure for the issuance of a declaration in regard to this government's attitude as to the disposition to be made of Palestine. This emanates naturally from the Zionist element of the Jews.

13. Ibid. (p. 385)
14. *Louis Marshall Champion of Liberty, Selected Papers & Addresses,* Edited by Charles Resnikoff, Vol. II (pp. 718-19)

My judgment is that we should go very slowly in announcing a policy for three reasons:

First, we are not at war with Turkey and therefore should avoid any appearance of favoring taking territory from that Empire by force.

Second, the Jews are by no means a unit in the desire to reestablish their race as an independent people, to favor one or the other faction would seem to be unwise.

Third, many Christian sects and individuals would undoubtedly resent turning the Holy Land over to the absolute control of the race credited with the death of Christ.

For practical purposes I do not think we need go further than the first reason given since that is ample ground for declining to announce a policy in regard to the final disposition of Palestine.

Faithfully yours,
Robert Lansing [15]

The Secretary of State to President Wilson
Washington, February 28, 1918

My dear Mr. President:

The Zionist Committee [16] through its secretary has sent me the letter which I attach hereto. This Committee makes two requests:

1) That passports be issued to representatives of the Committee to proceed to Palestine via London or Paris as a part of the Commission composed of representatives of the Zionist organization of England which is acting with the sanction of the British government.

2) That this Department recognize a Zionist Medical Unit composed of from thirty-five to forty-five persons. This unit is to proceed to Palestine to render service to the civilian population there.

15. *The Lansing Papers*, Vol. II (p. 71)
16. Referring to the Provisional Executive Committee for General Zionist Affairs

I hesitate to accede to these requests in view of the following considerations:

1) This government has never accepted Mr. Balfour's pronouncement with reference to the future of Palestine and has expressly refrained from accrediting consular agents to that territory, in which action the British government has entirely acquiesced.

2) This Government is not at war with Turkey.

3) A possible embarrassment may arise on account of the presence in Palestine of individuals, even though their errand is one of mercy, sponsored by an organization having distinctly political aims.

I should be grateful to you if you would advise me of your views with reference to this communication from the Zionist Committee.

Sincerely yours,
Robert Lansing [17]

---

17. *The Lansing Papers*, Vol. II (p. 107-108) (The President did give the authorization.)

Chapter 3

LOUIS D. BRANDEIS AS THE PUBLIC ZIONIST LEADER

Throughout many years Brandeis had been to a great extent separated from Jews. However, a spark for Jewish aspirations must have been glowing in his heart.

". . . Sometimes in the late nineties he wrote a letter to his wife from a Milwaukee hotel calling her attention to a magazine article on the colonization of Palestine and his belief that there was something good in the idea." [1]

The garment strike of 1910 must have influenced his life to a certain degree. The garment industry was an immigrant industry consisting mostly of Jews. He evidently began to think in terms of World Jewry.

Louis D. Brandeis' uncle, Louis Dembitz, for whom Brandeis was named ("D" for Dembitz), was privileged, at the Chicago Republican Convention in 1860, to be one of the three nominators of Abraham Lincoln. Dembitz was known as the Jewish scholar of the South. He was a devoted Zionist: three times elected as Vice President of the Federation of American Zionists. His article, "The Redemption of Palestine," was printed in the October 1901 issue of the *Maccabean*, the official Zionist publication.

Brandeis was very fond of his uncle and his affection might have planted seeds of sympathy for Zionism.

In the fall of 1910, the Zionist leader, Jacob De Haas, editor of the *Boston Jewish Advocate*, interviewed Brandeis about his fight in connection with the Mass. Savings Bank Insurance Law to give the wage earners an opportunity for cheap insurance.

". . . At the close of the insurance discussion the writer

1. *Louis D. Brandeis—A Biographical Sketch,* Jacob De Haas (p. 51)

14

(De Haas) ventured to identify the Boston attorney with the Louisville uncle for whom he was named . . .

". . . It was in explanation of our esteem of Louis Dembitz that we proceeded in the next hour to unfold the epic story of Theodor Herzl, the founder of the Zionist movement. That story told chapter by chapter in a series of interviews during the following winter, coupled with the capacity for the ideal which he had found in the needle workers of New York, opened to Brandeis new vistas." [2]

". . . He studied the footnotes as well as the printed pages of Jewish history and made the Zionist idea his own. In 1911 and 1912, while he was daily going through the tumult of his public role as 'People's Attorney', he snatched odd hours in which he gave close application to Jewish matters." [3]

". . . There was no public occasion for the presentation of opinion during 1911 and 1912, though during both years Brandeis made some contributions to Zionist funds and attended several meetings. His first Zionist utterances were at a meeting of the Boston New Century Club." [4]

Already in 1910 Brandeis publicly expressed his sympathy for Zionism in an interview, printed in the *Jewish Advocate*, New England's Jewish weekly, in its issue of December 9, 1910.

". . . In response to a question regarding his interest in the movement looking towards a revival of the Jewish State in Palestine, Mr. Brandeis said, 'I have a great deal of sympathy for the movement, and am deeply interested in the outcome of the propaganda. The so-called dreamers are entitled to the respect and appreciation of the entire Jewish people.' "

". . . I believe the Jews can be just as much of a priest people today as they ever were in the prophetic days." [*]

Brandeis' first public act of participation in Zionist activities

2. *Louis D. Brandeis—A Biographical Sketch*, Jacob De Haas (p. 51-52)
3. Ibid. (p. 53)
4. Ibid. (p. 53)
[*] It is rather astounding that Mr. Jonathan Shapiro interprets a quotation by Mr. Brandeis in the above-mentioned interview as proof that Brandeis was at that time opposed to Zionism (see his article about Brandeis in the *American Jewish Historical Quarterly*, December 25, 1965). The quotation reads as follows: ". . . This country demands that its sons and daughters whatever their race, however intense or diverse their reli-

was his chairmanship at a reception for Nahum Sokolow in Boston, March 1913. Sokolow, later President of the World Zionist Organization, was then touring the U.S. for the cause. In his book on Zionism, Sokolow refers to Brandeis:

". . . The statesmanship, the genius for organization, and the beneficient personal influence of the Hon. L. D. Brandeis, Judge of the Supreme Court, has raised, strengthened and secured in every direction the position of American Zionism not only in America, but also has increased its prestige and dignity abroad." [5]

". . . Brandeis' Zionist leadership and his influence in America equals almost that of Herzl in this hemisphere." [6]

In a letter, dated April 26, 1913, to Dr. Joseph Shohan, Secretary of the then just organized Zion Organization of Greater Boston, Brandeis writes:

"I thank you for your letter of the 24th notifying me of my election to the Board of Directors of the Zion Association of Greater Boston. I fear very much that my other engagements would not permit me to give to the work of the Board the time that a Director should give, and I dislike very much to appear as one of that great class of directors who do not direct." [7]

Deep in his heart, Brandeis must have felt that he owed a debt for having been aloof from his people for so many years. He seemingly waited for a call to take over the leadership, not of a single branch, but of the entire movement. He was said

gious connections be politically merely American citizens." Mr. Shapiro fails to inform his readers that the cited quotation which consists of six lines is taken out of an interview of 260 lines which is headlined: "Louis Dembitz Brandeis sympathizes with Zionism and believes in the Theory of a Jewish Mission." Mr. Shapiro goes even further: he tries to prove that Brandeis entered the Zionist arena because it was essential for his political success. It takes great audacity to accuse Brandeis, the Prince of humanity and Jewish renaissance, that he used Zionism to advance his political career. If he were not so confused, Mr. Shapiro would realize that if Brandeis had planned to use the Jewish community for his personal advancement he would, in those years, have joined the anti-Zionists and not the Zionists.

5. *History of Zionism,* Vol. II (p. 80)
6. Ibid. (p. 355)
7. *Brandeis Papers* (Reel 3) (Zionist Archives and Library)

to have once remarked: "I am in a hurry because I must make up for lost time."

On July 23, 1914, Dr. Schmarya Levin, in behalf of the Actions Comité of the World Zionist Organization and Louis Lipsky, in behalf of the Federation of American Zionists, issued a call to an extraordinary conference of representatives to be held at the Hotel Marseille, New York City, on August 30th. The aim of this conference was to maintain the integrity of the World Zionist Movement and to rescue the "Yishuv" from disintegration. It was just at that time that De Haas appealed to Brandeis to take over the leadership of the movement.

In a letter, dated August 26, 1914, De Haas writes to him:

Dear Mr. Brandeis:

I am loath to further disturb your vacation but I would call your attention to the importance of the circular which you have received from the Federation of American Zionists. I would very much like to know whether you will attend the meeting to be held in New York this Sunday. If that should not be the case, I should like to have your authority for proposing your name as the Chairman or Directing Head of the Committee which will have to take charge at this time of practically the whole Zionist Movement.

I know that this is asking a great deal of you, but I feel that the unique circumstances warrant my asking such a sacrifice of time and convenience. There are likely to arise a great number of demands in which only a man of your capacity and influence can be of service.

Not only the Colonist Movement is at stake, but indeed the welfare of seven-tenths of the Jewish race is involved. It is not only a question of our own institutions and their future, but the coolest and most able head is needed to devise plans whereby we shall be able to save the body of Jews at the end of the war. We already know what we can expect of men of the Schiff type. I think that the Jews of America will accept your leader-

17

ship in this crisis, and that an army of zealous workers will be at your disposal to carry out the manifold policy that in my judgement the situation demands. It is not too much to say that everything depends on American Jewry and that Jewry has to be led right.

I am leaving for Nashua, N.H., and mail until Saturday noon will reach me if sent to my office. If you wish you can reach me by telegraph c/o Dr. M. Benmosche, Nashua, N.H., or by telegram at the same address.

With very kind regards, I remain,

Very truly yours.

J. De Haas [8]

Brandeis agreed to be nominated and he was unanimously elected as Chairman of the Provisional Executive Committee for General Zionist Affairs. It was the beginning of a new era in the Zionist Movement.

The following remarks were made by Brandeis upon his acceptance of the office of Chairman of the Provisional Zionist Committee on August 30, 1914:

". . . Throughout long years which represent my own life, I have been to a great extent separated from Jews. I am very ignorant in things Jewish. But recent experiences, public and professional, have taught me this: I find Jews possessed of those very qualities which we of the twentieth century seek to develop in our struggle for justice and democracy; a deep moral feeling which makes them capable of noble acts; a deep sense of brotherhood of man; and a high intelligence, the fruit of three thousand years of civilization. These experiences have made me feel that the Jewish people have something which should be saved for the world; that the Jewish people should be preserved, and that it is our duty to pursue that method of saving which most promises success . . ." [9]

There had been instant agreement at the conference that the glamor of the name of the "People's Attorney" would lend

8. *Brandeis Papers* (Reel 3)
9. *Brandeis on Zionism,* Edited by Solomon Goldman (p. 43-44)

luster to the cause that needed great aid, but it occurred to no one, and seemingly not even to De Haas, that the new leader would throw himself into the work—lock, stock and barrel—that he would carry his work day by day, hour by hour, turning over details to nobody before he himself had checked them and reached a conclusion.

In a letter to De Haas, at that time Chairman of the Zionist Bureau for New England, dated January 25, 1915, Brandeis asked him:

"Please arrange that I receive not later than the 5th of each month a report covering the activities of the Zionist Bureau during the preceding month.

"I should be glad if you would give some care to the form of the report, so that it may be possible by comparison of the reports from month to month, to note readily the progress that has been made in each line of activity, and serve as a current reference to the achievements of the Bureau." [10]

In a letter to Dr. Schmarya Levin, who represented the World Zionist Movement in the United States, dated March 1, 1915, Brandeis writes:

My dear Dr. Levin:

I write to confirm the request made at the meeting of the Provisional Committee on Thursday last, namely:

First: That you should prepare at the earliest possible moment a draft of a letter to be signed by me, in which I shall make to the Actions Comité a comprehensive report of the work of our Committee during the six months ending February 28th; and a statement of the present conditions of the organization in America.

Second: That you prepare weekly thereafter a draft of a letter to be signed by me, reporting to the Actions Comité such part of the work of the Committee, or of occurrences during the preceding week which it may seem proper to communicate.

Third: That you submit a list of persons or organiza-

10. *Brandeis Papers* (Reel 3)

tions to whom a copy of the letter to the Actions Comité should be sent . . ." [11]

In a letter from Boston to E. W. Lewin-Epstein [12] in New York, dated March 1, 1915, Brandeis writes: ". . . Confirming my conversation with you, Mr. Lipsky and Mr. Pearlstein yesterday concerning the efficiency of the work of our Committee, and the arrangements then made:

"First: You will daily, except Saturday and Sunday, come to the administrative offices of the Committee at 3:00 P.M. for an hour or such part thereof as may be necessary and there take up and dispose of, in executive session with Mr. Lipsky and Mr. Pearlstein, all of the matters requiring attention from day to day, it being the understanding that Mr. Lipsky and Mr. Pearlstein will arrange so that during that hour they and you will be undisturbed.

"As to Sunday: I assume that you will make with Mr. Lipsky and Mr. Pearlstein such arrangements as may be desirable for conferences on that day . . ." [13]

When Brandeis began his leadership he studied Zionism as he had studied gas, insurance and railroading, the three important problems in his legal philosophy.

In a letter to Professor Richard Gottheil, dated January 14, 1915, Brandeis writes:

". . . I hope you will be able to make a report to me soon embodying the results of your investigation into Herzl, and other negotiations with various powers. I realize how much you have been hampered in getting material from abroad bearing on this matter, but I hope you will let me have soon whatever is available." [14]

In a letter to Professor Gottheil, dated December 29, 1915, Brandeis writes: ". . . Have you any data concerning the draft of the charter which was prepared in Herzl's time in connection with his negotiations with the British government and the Sul-

11. Ibid. (Reel 5)
12. Lewin-Epstein was the Treasurer of the Provisional Committee.
13. *Brandeis Papers* (Reel 5)
14. *Brandeis Papers* (Reel 3)

tan? Please let me have whatever information or papers you can give me on this subject." [15]

As soon as he took over the leadership, he was evidently convinced that you need a strong organization in order to play the master stroke in the restoration of Zion. He therefore kept on repeating his appeal on every occasion:

"Organize, organize, organize, until every Jewish American must stand up and be counted, counted with us, or prove himself wittingly or unwittingly one of the few who are against their own people."

In his address at the 18th Annual Convention of the Federation of American Zionists, held in Boston, at the end of June 1915, Mr. Brandeis again emphasized the importance of concentrating on organization work in order to strengthen the Zionist ranks:

". . . We recognize, as every one of you must recognize with profound satisfaction, that the day is very near, which Rabbi Berlin prayed for, the day when we shall no longer have to speak of Zionists but of Jews, because practically all Jews will be Zionists." [16]

No wonder that early in the morning Brandeis was already at his desk for Zionist work. He was the one to make decisions and to give instructions, but at the same time to ignore nobody, to cooperate with everybody, and to be in touch not only with every leader, but with anybody who wanted to help the movement.

In a special delivery letter from Brandeis in Boston to Dr. Wise, dated February 20, 1915, Brandeis writes:

My dear Dr. Wise:

First: I am delighted to hear your report of the victory in Cincinnati.

Second: I hope you will be able to make definite arrangements to come by motor from Exeter so as to make the 1:00 a.m. train Wednesday night to New York, and I will take the same train. It seems to me important

15. Ibid. (Reel 3)
16. *Maccabean,* July 1915

that we should have a chance to talk out fully in conference before the meeting many matters relating to Zionist affairs:

1. You, Dr. Magnes, and I, possibly with some others, relief ship matters.[17]

2. You, Dr. Magnes, Dr. Levin, Professor Gottheil and I, the Zionist political questions.

3. You, Miss Szold, Mr. Lipsky, Mr. Pearlstein and I, questions of propaganda and organization.

Third: Your success in Buffalo is grand and shows how important it is to have you do the speaking on such occasions." [18]

In connection with the relief ship, "Vulcan," which carried nine hundred tons of foodstuffs, it is worthwhile to cite the following letter from the Secretary of the Navy:

Washington, March 9, 1915

My dear Mr. Brandeis:

I have the pleasure of acknowledging your kind letter of the 5th inst. voicing appreciation by the Jews of America for the service rendered their brethren in Palestine by this Department. The Navy Department has held itself in readiness at all times to render assistance where assistance was needed, and the President was much pleased when he learned that it would be possible for the carrier "Vulcan" to provide facilities for the transportation of supplies and medicines to the suffering in Palestine on her forthcoming voyage to the Mediterranean with provisions and coal for American ships now stationed in those waters.

I am much gratified myself that the Department has been able to cooperate with your Committee to this extent and, as a result, we have another instance of a serv-

17. The Steamer "Vulcan" transported much needed medicines and tools to the Jews in Palestine.
18. *Brandeis Papers* (Reel 3)

ice organized for purely military functions rendering valuable aid to the cause of humanity.

With expression of my high esteem and kind regards, believe me,

Yours very sincerely,
Josephus Daniels [19]

In connection with this relief work it was Brandeis who used his influence with the State Department. The following letter dated June 3, 1915, was written by Brandeis to Albert H. Putney, Chief Division "Near East," Department of State, Washington, D.C.:

Dear Sir:

You will recall my conference with you, Mr. Carr and Secretary Phillips about a month ago, which resulted in a cable to our Ambassador in Russia concerning collections to be made there for the relief of Jewish sufferers in Palestine, and to be transmitted to me. You will kindly let me know whether any communication has been received in relation to the matter.

Yours very truly,
Louis D. Brandeis [20]

A very important task which then confronted the Provisional Committee was to prevent the destruction of the Jewish Settlement in Palestine, which was in great danger during the dictatorship of Kemal Pasha.

The following communication from the Secretary of State, William Jennings Bryan, and the Ambassador's reply show the influence that Brandeis exerted:

Telegram

The Secretary of State to the Ambassador in Turkey (Morgenthau):

Washington, April 29, 1915

19. *Brandeis Papers* (Reel 2)
20. Ibid. (Reel 2)

633. Department April 27, and your 608, April 27. Urge Turkish Government to protect both Armenians and Zionists.

Bryan [21]

Telegram

The Ambassador to Turkey (Morgenthau) to the Secretary of State:
Constantinople, May 2, 1915
624. Your 633 . . . We have succeeded in suspending movement against Zionists and secured permission for their representative Jacobson to leave Turkey instead of being expelled.
American Ambassador [22]

The following letters will show how Brandeis, day by day, hour by hour, was trying to find ways and means to strengthen the Zionist Organization and to increase its membership:

New York, April 30, 1915

Louis D. Brandeis, Esq.
Dear Sir:
Enclosed I beg to hand you report of the Committee appointed by you to consider plans for mobilizing and training Jewish high school boys, and those of the same age outside of high school, along the lines of Zionist sentiment coupled with physical development and Boy Scout discipline.
Faithfully yours,
Ralph E. Fleisher
(Counselor at Law) [23]

---

21. *U.S. Papers Relating to Foreign Relations of the United States* 1915 (p. 980)
22. Ibid. (p. 981)
23. *Brandeis Papers* (Reel 3)

New York, April 27, 1915

Mr. Louis Brandeis
Boston, Mass.

Dear Mr. Brandeis:

As you suggested, I have gone around quietly and tried to get supporters among young college men for our College Zionist Association. I have already a substantial number of promises from men of high caliber, and will be able to report at our next meeting on the 2nd of May.

William   Rosenblatt [24]

In a letter dated April 7, 1915, to Henry Hurwitz, New York City, Brandeis writes:

Dear Mr. Hurwitz:

I am much gratified at receiving the pledge from the various members who met on April 4, 1915 at 600 Madison Avenue, and who have agreed to volunteer their services to the Zionist cause, placing themselves at my disposal for the period of six months to act as I direct.

I desire to give careful consideration to the possibilities of utilizing the services of the several men in specific work, and will write you later my conclusions in this respect.

Meanwhile, however, there is one class of work which each of the men named is requested to perform continuously during the period of six months, and which they should undertake at once; namely, by personal propaganda among those with whom they come in contact to secure adherents to the Zionist cause, and, if possible, enrollment as members of one of the Zionist societies. Special effort should be made by each to secure adherents of men in his own profession, and to develop, so far as possible, a plan for his personal work in this direction. All of the men named are university men, and the enrollment of membership would be naturally as

24. Ibid. (Reel 3)

25

members of the University Zionist Society about to be formed.

We should have from each of the men a report on the first day of each month covering the activities during the preceding month, which should list the names and occupations of the persons whom it has sought to win for the Zionist cause, and the results of the attempts in each instance. The study of these lists will be made as presented with a view to aiding the propaganda work. An effort will also be undertaken to aid the work by bringing the men into connection with other Zionists in their profession, with whom they can cooperate in the work of propaganda.[25]

In a letter from Boston to Judge Mack, New York City, dated April 2, 1915, Brandeis writes: ". . . Hope you will arrange to attend our college men's conference with Kallen, Gottheil, Hurwitz and others at Aeolian Building, ten o'clock, Sunday morning. I shall be at the Zionist headquarters tomorrow morning. Should be glad to have you at Saturday night's meeting, but do not consider that so important as the Sunday morning conference." [26]

A letter to Brandeis from the Menorah Society, Minneapolis, Minnesota, October 7, 1914:

My Esteemed Sir:
The Menorah Society of the University of Minnesota, having heard that you are contemplating a tour of the West, extends to you a most hearty invitation to address the student body of the University of Minnesota and the members of the Menorah Society in particular.

Should it not be your present intention to include Minneapolis in your itineary, we must humbly ask you to change your route, so as to include our city.

A few words from you would go extensively toward

25. *Brandeis Papers* (Reel 3)
26. Ibid. (Reel 5)

fostering a spirit of self-respect amongst our people. It is a foregone conclusion that amongst our young people and a good number of the old, anything bearing on Jewish ideals or Jewish culture is banal, not because Jewish ideals and Jewish culture in their estimation is not on a level with non-Jewish ideals, but simply because it is Jewish.

Out in the West your words are law, and we rejoice in your successes. We regard you as the recognized leader of American Jewry.

Thus, if you can possibly arrange to come to Minneapolis, you will fill a most heartfelt want in our community—the Jew will learn to respect himself, and the non-Jew will respect him because of the Jewish self-respect—which apparently is lacking.

With kindest personal regards, I am,

Very sincerely yours,
Alex Kanter [27]

A letter to Brandeis from Young Judea, dated January 1, 1915:

Dear Mr. Brandeis:

As a Zionist I am sure you will be interested in the work of Young Judea.

. . . Young Judea is a league of 175 junior Zionist clubs. In these clubs, under the guidance of volunteer leaders, we are imbued with Jewish national ideals. We study Jewish history and literature, sing Jewish songs, and debate on Zionism and Jewish problems.

This work has been going on for five years under the supervision and control of the Federation of American Zionists. Young Judea has been aptly termed "the insurance policy of the Zionist Movement."

. . . Some word of encouragement and advice from

27. *Brandeis Papers* (Reel 1)

you would materially assist us in our work. Trusting to hear from you and with Zion's greetings,

Sincerely yours,
Sundel Doniger
(Chairman Executive
Comm.) [28]

In a letter to Professor H. M. Kallen, Berkeley, California, dated February 10, 1915, Brandeis writes:

My dear Kallen:
I have considered most carefully yours of the first and have discussed it with Wise.
". . . I feel very strongly that our policy should be to avoid controversy and to win those who at present are indifferent. We can cover but a small part, with our present forces, of the field that is open to us. If we develop Zionism in those communities where its prospects are bright, we shall reap a much larger crop; and if our work is well done, Philipson and the like will be isolated and will shrivel up.
". . . I hope soon after you come East to have an opportunity to talk the situation over with you." [29]

In a letter from Boston, Mass., dated March 2, 1915, to Sylvan Robinson, New York City, Brandeis writes:

"My dear Mr. Robinson:
I was very glad to learn from the minutes of the Executive Committee meeting of the Federation of American Zionists on February 18th, which has just reached me, that the plan of propaganda, by means of private gatherings and home parties for the purpose of securing converts to the cause and eventual members of the organization, was accepted.

28. *Brandeis Papers* (Reel 1)
29. Ibid. (Reel 2)

The plans of your Committee seem to me eminently wise and promising; but I hope that it will not be left merely to the Zion Association to carry out its work. Your Committee and each of its members ought to make every endeavor to arrange for such private gatherings, and the time is ripe for such a course.

During the last six months the subject of Zionism has attracted considerable attention. It is looked upon now favorably in many quarters where it was formerly regarded with disfavor. But the ignorance concerning the cause is still very great. Such private gatherings as were suggested in the vote are the really effective means of removing that ignorance; and I feel that you are among the relatively few who are most competent to conduct such meetings.

I hope therefore that you will be able to give much time to arranging and conducting such gatherings between now and the summer vacation.

Very cordially yours,
Louis D. Brandeis
Chairman [30]

In a letter dated March 3, 1915, Bernard Rosenblatt writes to Brandeis: ". . . In regard to the matter of 'home gatherings' and small private affairs for Zionist membership, I may say that I have discussed the matter with Mrs. Rosenblatt and we hope to work out a definite plan within the next few days." [31]

In a letter, dated May 21, 1915, Benjamin Pearlstein, Administrative Secretary of the Provisional Committee reported to Brandeis:

"My dear Mr. Brandeis:

First: I was very sorry to learn from your night letter that you are not well, and that you are forced to cancel your various arrangements.

Second: Mr. Rosenblatt will call off the meeting at his

30. *Brandeis Papers* (Reel 3)
31. Ibid. (Reel 3)

father-in-law's home because he feels that only you can make an impression on the gentlemen who were expected to be present:

Third: In accordance with the letter that Wise is enclosing, the Provisional Committee's meeting of Monday evening will be postponed until such time as you can be present. When the Budget Committee met this afternoon, Dr. Wise felt that you ought to be present at the discussion of the budget, as it involved several radical steps . . .

. . . Sixth: I am enclosing a copy of a letter written to you by Rabbi Berlin,[32] and a copy which I have framed for you to sign; it if meets with your approval, kindly sign and mail . . .

. . . Eighth: I am enclosing a copy of a letter received from the Poale Zion,[33] inviting you to be present at a banquet for Mr. Kaplansky; I am also enclosing my reply and would suggest that you send a telegram of greetings.

. . . I shall be in the office tomorrow, in case you desire to wire me.

Trusting that you will soon be able to be with us again, I beg to remain with Zion's greetings." [34]

There is hardly a day when Brandeis has not some new ideas how to srengthen the organization. In a letter to Judge J. W. Mack, Mackinac Island, Michigan, dated August 17, 1915, he writes:

"My dear Judge Mack:

I understand that McCormack of the *Chicago Tribune* has been talked to in regard to the Congress and Zionism and that he says he will be glad to write on the subject after he has talked with some Chicago Jews of standing.

32. Rabbi Berlin was the leader of the "Mizrachi," the Orthodox Zionist Organization.
33. The Labor Zionist Organization
34. *Brandeis Papers* (Reel 2)

30

I hope that you will call him up on the telephone, if you are not to be in Chicago within the next few days, and talk with him on the subject, so that he may understand how important it is that the *Tribune* shall give ample publicity to the Movement." [35]

In a telegram dated October 23, 1915, Brandeis wires Secretary Robert Lansing, Department of State, Washington, D.C.: "Judge Mack of Chicago will call early Monday on urgent Palestine business. Hope you can see him then and give aid requested.[36]

There is no wonder that such devotion brought remarkable results:

The total receipts of the Provisional Committee for the period from June 30, 1915 to June 19, 1916, excluding transfer issues, totaled: $356,910.72.[37]

As already mentioned, when Brandeis took over the Zionist leadership in August, 1914, there were only twelve thousand enrolled members in the Federation of American Zionists. At the 22nd Annual Convention of the Zionist Organization of America, September 14-19, 1919, at Chicago, Illinois, the number of enrolled members was 176,658.[38]

"December 16, 1917, Baltimore, Maryland: Special Zionist Conference meets to discuss practical questions arising as a result of the British Declaration for a Jewish Home in Palestine. Conference called by Provisional Committee.

"Decided to launch campaign to raise one hundred million dollar fund for restoration of the Holy Land." [39]

His continuous work to build the organization did not prevent him from devoting just as much energy to all other problems of the movement, as for example, the American Jewish Congress and Hadassah.

Just as in 1915, Brandeis' approval of the American Jewish Congress was instantly followed by aggressive and effective

35. Ibid. (Reel 5)
36. Ibid. (Reel 5)
37. *Maccabean*, October 1916
38. *American Jewish Year Book* 5681
39. Ibid. 5678

31

action, so in 1917, did his acceptance of the principle of the Jewish Legion for Palestine lead immediately to active recruiting. It was the leadership of Brandeis which turned the project of a Jewish Congress from a wishful aspiration to an actuality against the passionate opposition of both the right and the left. Elections were held by every Jewish community throughout the land, and the first session of the American Jewish Congress opened on December 15, 1918. In his statements for the Jewish Congress, Brandeis stressed the point that one could not have it both ways: that one could not accept democracy as a citizen of the country and reject it as a member of one of its Jewish communities.

In a telegram, dated December 31, 1915, Wise reports to Brandeis:

"Richards claims absolutely unable to pay most urgent bills. Requires minimum two hundred immediately for current office expenses. Shall Provisional advance that sum. Please wire." [40]

In a letter to Brandeis in Louisville, Kentucky, dated January 3, 1916, Wise writes:

"I had your telegram and have, in compliance with your request, forwarded my check for two hundred dollars to Mr. Richards . . ." [41]

In a letter dated July 16, 1915, Louis Lipsky, Chairman of the Executive Committee, Federation of American Zionists, writes to Brandeis:

"Dear Mr. Brandeis:
Mr. Cohen told me for Mr. De Haas that you had agreed to the Ruttenberg proposition relating to the agitation to be conducted for the Congress among the Jewish socialistic organizations. I saw Mr. Ruttenberg and Dr. Elsberg today.
It was agreed between us that $500 should be advanced to Dr. Elsberg and Mr. Ruttenberg as representatives of the National Socialistic Agitation Committee, and that they were to regard the matter as confidential, the

40. *Brandeis Papers* (Reel 3)
41. Ibid. (Reel 3)

source of the contribution to be known only to Dr. Elsberg and Mr. Ruttenberg who were to report in detail to this office.

I am to call up Dr. Elsberg on Monday morning to inform him if and when the payment will be made.

The National Socialistic Agitation Committee has been formed by Mr. Ruttenberg with the following Executive Committee: Ruttenberg, Schitlowsky, Elsberg, Ehrenreich and Isaak A. Hourvich. The Finance Committee, however, is composed of Elsberg, Klimenko, Kopolof and Ruttenberg. There is also a Press Committee on which are Syrkin, Schitlowsky, and a large number of active journalists who have been won over to the cause (I have intimated to Dr. Elsberg and Mr. Ruttenberg that it would be advisable not to admit Mr. Houvrich into full confidence).

The National Socialistic Agitation Committee has adopted the following objectives: To organize all radical socialistic elements and to have them send delegates to the Jewish Congress on the following platform:

1) National equal rights for the Jews in all lands.

2) An independent political home for the Jewish people in Palestine.

These elements are to be organized to participate in a convention of all radical Jewish working men's organizations which is to be held early in September, where the question of participation in the Jewish Congress is to be decided. In the meantime, the National Socialistic Agitation Committee will establish a press bureau, and begin a strong agitation among the rank and file of the organizations that are now, through their officers, not favorably disposed toward the above mentioned program. A group of six writers, exclusive of Mr. Ruttenberg, have pledged themselves to write in their newspapers articles on subjects selected by Mr. Ruttenberg, and on no other subjects. Mr. Ruttenberg will issue a statement; there will be no manifestoes, etc., and direct correspondence with individual societies will be taken up.

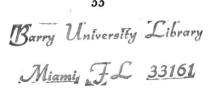

Should the National Arbeiter Convention reject the program as given, the nationalistic forces will withdraw and form a body to act with a democratic nationalistic Jewish congress.

Mr. Ruttenberg does not rely upon Meyer London for work in the Arbeiter Ring, but believes if Morris Hilquith were to become interested, he could be depended upon. Mr. Ruttenberg believes that the opponents of our program, may, in an emergency, abandon democratic aspirations in favor of preventing the Zionists from making, as they say, political capital out of the Congress. This attitude may lead the old-time leaders to a coalition with the American Jewish Committee, which, however, may be prevented by the publicity the National Socialistic Agitation Committee will give to the whole controversy.

I await your further instructions." [42]

In a letter to Bernard Richards, Secretary of the Jewish Congress Organization Committee, dated September 22, 1915, Brandeis writes:

". . .When I attend the Conference called by Mr. Kraus for October 3rd, I shall want to have with me a schedule showing:

1) All the organizations which have specifically declared in favor of a Congress, and the number of their members.

2) All the cities in which there have been general meetings, like that recently held in Kansas City, in favor of a Conference, with a definite designation in respect to each city as to what organizations participated in the meeting, and the number of persons.

3) A specific statement showing in respect to such organizations as may be supposed to be friendly to a Conference, like the I.O.B.A., Y.M.H.A., etc., what lodges or subsidiary societies have expressed themselves definitely in favor of a Congress.

42. *Brandeis Papers* (Reel 5)

I trust that the activities during the next ten days will be such as to make the list a very long one." [43]

Brandeis insisted that the American Jewish Committee must agree to call a democratic Congress which should consider civil rights for Jews everywhere and the right of the Jews to a homeland in Palestine in particular.

Hadassah,[44] since its inception in 1912 had been closely tied up with the Zionist life of Brandeis. It was when the Zionist Medical Unit was being organized that Brandeis came into close contact with Hadassah.

In a letter to Brandeis, dated April 14, 1915, Henrietta Szold writes:

> "The Central Committee of Hadassah held its first meeting last evening since we received your kind letter of March 24th, containing your generous offer to help us substantially with the publication of our Bulletin.
>
> The Central Committee wishes me to express to you its appreciation of your kindness. We agree with you that the usefulness of the Bulletin will be much increased by having it appear in letter type . . ." [45]

In another letter to Brandeis, dated May 18, 1915, Miss Szold writes: "The members of the Central Committee of Hadassah have requested me to put a petition before you. We know that the convention in Boston is going to tax your time and your strength, and yet we venture the hope that you will honor the Hadassah sub-convention with your presence and your word in its closing hour, at least . . ." [46]

In a letter to Eugene Meyer, Jr., dated November 5, 1915, Brandeis writes:

> "First: I am in receipt of yours of the 3rd. I am sorry to learn that we are to get only $2,500 from Mr. Guggen-

43. Ibid. (Reel 5)
44. The Women's Zionist Organization
45. *Brandeis Papers* (Reel 5)
46. *Brandeis Papers* (Reel 5)

heim. I trust that you and Dr. Wise are making progress elsewhere.

Second: The money is being raised to be loaned to the Palestinian planters, upon the best security available. I suggest that you have him send the check to you as Treasurer of the Palestinian Loan Committee, and that the funds be deposited at present in the bank in an account in your name as Treasurer.

Third: I am to be in New York on Thursday, November 11th and Friday, November 12th. Thursday evening I have an engagement, but I should be glad to have you dine with me at the City Club on Friday evening, at 7 o'clock, or dine with you, whichever you prefer, at some place where we may sit down and discuss particularly Palestinian financial problems . . .[47]

What Nordau Thinks of Brandeis

In a letter dated January 10, 1916, Henry Hurwitz, Editorial Chief of the *Menorah Journal*, published by the Intercollegiate Menorah Association, writes to Brandeis:

I have just received a letter from Dr. Nordau,[48] from Madrid, in which he says: 'The controversy of Mr. Brandeis with the American Jewish Committee is of very far reaching importance. The former triumphs easily by his straightforwardness, his close logic, his broadmindedness, and his sound democratic principles. His victory promises to become the point of departure of a serious permanent organization of American Judaism which is bound to be soon followed by that of all other important Jewries of the Old World. And such an organization is the obligatory preliminary condition of a satisfactory solution to the Jewish problem. With all my heart, I wish that good and noble Jew, Mr. Brandeis and his followers, God Speed.' [49]

47. Ibid. (Reel 5)
48. Dr. Max Nordau was a very prominent Zionist leader in Europe.
49. *Brandeis Papers* (Reel 5)

In his letter to Hurwitz, dated January 11, 1916, Brandeis writes:

First: Thank you for your letter of the 10th containing the quotation from Dr. Nordau.

Second: I presume you have seen Judge Mack, and heard about our interesting meeting in Cincinnati and from Kallen about the Knights of Zion Convention.

Third: I was considerably disturbed by reports that have come to me of the inactivity of the University Zionist Society. Please let me have a full report in regard to it, and let me know what you think can be done to get from it the help which we expected . . ." [50]

Until June 1916, when Brandeis was appointed by President Wilson and then confirmed by the Senate as Justice of the Supreme Court, his Zionist leadership was a public one.

One of his last letters during that period, dated April 3, 1916, is addressed to Hon. Robert Lansing, Secretary of State:

"Dear Sir:

We beg to inform you that Mr. Julius Berger, of Berlin, is acting on behalf of our Committee in making investigations of the conditions of the Jews suffering through the war in occupied territory. Mr. Berger is now in Warsaw, and he would request the courtesy of your Department to advise Mr. Hernando de Soto, American Consul at Warsaw, by cable, that Mr. Berger is officially representing our Committee, and to assist him, insofar as it is compatible with the rules of the State Department, to forward reports to us on conditions he finds there.

We shall be pleased to pay the charges in connection with these cables upon receipt of a bill from you.

Thanking you in advance, I beg to remain,

Very truly yours,
L. D. Brandeis" [51]

---

50. *Brandeis Papers* (Reel 5)
51. Ibid. (Reel 2)

Chapter 4

JUSTICE BRANDEIS AS THE SILENT ZIONIST LEADER

The Zionist leadership of Brandeis from August 30, 1914, to June 1921, when he was defeated at the Cleveland Convention by the adherents of Dr. Weizmann, consisted of two parts: his Public Leadership and his Silent Leadership.

In 1916, when he was appointed Justice to the Supreme Court, he resigned from a few Jewish organizations, but not from the Provisional Zionist Committee. He only changed his title from Chairman to Honorary Chairman. He continued his day by day, hour by hour, Zionist work as the Silent Leader.

A most phenomenal part in Brandeis' character, something which is very rare to find among national and international leaders, was his hatred for publicity, his distaste for political spotlight. So much in public limelight, he was extremely reluctant to shed light on his own self. This lack of publicity must have had a great deal to do with his defeat at the Cleveland Convention. Some of the delegates definitely did not know that all the Zionist victories, both social and political, could never have been achieved without Brandeis.

During his silent leadership, not less than during his public leadership, his secretary kept on asking the Central Zionist Office, "Will you be good enough to send me, for Mr. Brandeis, an additional supply of letterheads." [1] During his silent leadership something additional, something new was added to his Zionist work: his leading role in directing the Zionist affairs in the field of international diplomacy.

It was Brandeis who succeeded in interesting President Wilson in the Jewish aspirations for Palestine in spite of the fact that almost all who surrounded him were opposed to the Zionist

1. *Brandeis Papers* (Reel 2)

Movement. The President sympathized fully with Brandeis' Zionist views. Thanks to his sympathy and the President's constant reliance on the Justice's judgment, it was Brandeis who assured the making of the Balfour Declaration. But the Balfour Declaration was only a promise. This promise had to be translated into action, and it was Justice Brandeis who had to cover a very big road to the Peace Conference in Paris and the Allied Council at San Remo, a road full of obstacles; among them, The Sykes-Picot Agreement, the King-Crane Commission, and the hostility to Zionism of Colonel House and the Secretary of State, Robert Lansing.

Only seven weeks that Brandeis did not participate daily in Zionist work

The following is the first statement by Brandeis on Zionism after his appointment to the Supreme Court. It was made in acknowledgment of a testimonial signed by 10,000 Zionists and presented to him on the occasion of his sixtieth birthday on November 13, 1916:

"The few years which cover my real activity in Zionist affairs have been rich in their gifts to me. They brought me understanding and happiness.

... The last seven weeks which have separated me from that daily participation in the work of the Zionists, have not left me without knowledge of what is occurring. Conferences with Jacob De Haas, who was active originally in bringing me into the Cause and upon whose wisdom and devotion and experience I have relied so much, and daily reports from the office have kept me in touch with what is going on. There may be many details which I do not know with that accuracy with which I knew when I was at the Zionist office every week and had Zionist conferences every day. But I do feel, in a general way, fully advised, and the aloofness of those seven weeks, the distance incident to residence in Washington may perhaps enable me to see with greater clear-

39

ness our opportunities, our necessities, and our dangers.

I feel more than ever that the opportunities are very great, greater than at any time in eighteen centuries. The world is with us, that is, the non-Jewish world. Whether the Jewish world will be with us, will depend very largely upon the Zionists themselves." [2]

Brandeis Participates Silently at the Pittsburgh Convention

". . . By one of those sudden inspirations that come unexpectedly at dramatic moments, someone who just then espied Justice Brandeis sitting alone in the gallery above, sprang to his feet and waving his hand frantically in that direction, began to cheer.

What happened the next instant will long be remembered by all present as one of the most wonderful and stimulating experiences through which they had ever passed. The whole Convention, 500 strong, sprang to their feet and broke into a demonstration of unequalled fervor and earnestness. They shouted 'Hadad' until they were hoarse. They applauded; they sang; they stood upon the seats and wildly waved their hats; they called Brandeis by name and made the heavens ring with their cheers. It was as though a hurricane, elemental in its might, had swept through them. And it was those few moments more than anything else that occurred throughout the Convention that served to create the new "Zionist Organization of America." The conferences, the resolutions, the constitution, the motions and the amendments, all these but supplied the body; it was that historic demonstration that breathed a soul into the clay."

The Silent Leader at his Daily Zionist Work

In a letter dated February 7, 1918, to Beny Lewis, Los Angeles, California, Brandeis writes:

2. *Brandeis on Zionism*, Solomon Goldman (p. 110-111)
3. "Two of the 'High Spots' at the Pittsburgh Convention," Emanuel Neuman, *Maccabean*, August 1918

"My thanks for your letter, and will you kindly express to Rev. J. Weinstock my appreciation.

Please send me hereafter on the first of each month a report stating:

1. Number of new members added during the preceeding month.

2. Amount collected for Restoration Fund during the preceding month.

3. Number of shekels sold during the preceding month.[4]

In a letter to Mrs. Guggenheimer, dated March 18, 1918, Brandeis writes:

"Let me thank you for sending me the Hadassah report.

The percentage of gain over the preceding year is appreciable, but the number of regular members is so small as to indicate that the plan of operation must be defective.

You should have in New York as many thousands as you now have hundreds; indeed as many tens of thousands.

I have talked this over recently with Mr. De Haas and wish you would confer with him.

The women should furnish at least half our membership." [5]

In a letter to Morris Margulies, Chairman, Greater New York Campaign Committee, P.R.F.,[6] dated May 14, 1918, Brandeis writes: "I am glad to have this report of your Committee's accomplishments to May 1st, and look forward to its doubling the amount before June 1st.

"Let me also express the hope that your Committee will

4. *De Haas Papers* (Reel 3)
5. Ibid. (Reel 3)
6. Palestine Restoration Fund

41

record at least 50,000 shekel payers before that date, through its affiliations." [7]

In a letter to Walter E. Mayer (transmitted by E. W. Lewin-Epstein), dated April 10, 1918, Brandeis writes:

"My dear Walter:

I was indeed glad to hear through Felix that you had gone to Palestine as Dr. Weizmann's aide, and now comes your letter from Atranto. You will, I am sure, be of much help also to the American Medical Unit, and the knowledge and understanding gained in Palestine will be of inestimable advantage to the Cause upon your return from Palestine.

Let us have from time to time full reports—and gather comprehensively from observation, men and books, all the facts and opinions which may be of value to us here in enlisting the interest of American Jews and in guiding our policies." [8]

In a letter to Rabbi Solomon Sadowsky, Rochester, New York, dated July 5, 1918, Brandeis writes: "Let me thank you for your kind letter. I trust that you will not rest until every member of your congregation is not only a shekel payer, but an affiliated member of the Zionist Organization." [9]

In a letter to Samuel W. Herzlinger, Brooklyn, New York, dated July 16, 1918, Brandeis writes:

Let me thank you for the photographs and for your very kind letter.

Bear in mind that there is much you can do for the Zionist Cause. Our great task in America now is to strengthen the Organization: "Men, Money and Discipline" are the essentials.

Make it your daily work to gain some members for

7. *De Haas Papers* (Reel 3)
8. *De Haas Papers* (Reel 3)
9. Ibid. (Reel 3)

the Zionist Organization and let us have a report once a month giving the names and addresses and occupations. [10]

In a letter to Mrs. Joseph Fels, New York City, dated August 22, 1918, Brandeis writes:

My dear Mrs. Fels:
You will remember our talk with the Zimbalists about the *Hatikvah* and their promise to prepare the record during the summer, so that it may be marketed in the Fall.
The summer is nearing the close and I hope this has not been overlooked.[11]

Telegram

August 26, 1918

Mr. Justice Louis D. Brandeis
Stoneleigh Court, Washington, D.C.

Wise has White House appointment Tuesday four. He will see you early morning.

Jacob De Haas [12]

Brandeis' Letter to Walter Meyer, October 26, 1918

My dear Walter:
I received today from Sam Lewisohn a check for $500 in his own account and a check for $1,000 from his father for the Zionist work in Palestine—for which we are indebted to you.
Thanks also for the copy of your letter to Ormsby-Gore. Dena has doubtless shown you my recent letter to G.[13]

10. Ibid. (Reel 3)
11. Ibid. (Reel 3)
12. Ibid. (Reel 3)
13. *De Haas Papers* (Reel 3)

Telegram

October 28, 1918

Dr. Harry Friedenwald
Baltimore, Maryland

Please be at Justice Brandeis' house Tuesday morning nine o'clock. Important.

De Haas [14]

Telegram

November 20, 1918

Jacob De Haas
New York City

Please have Wise see the letter from Chief before taking any action on seeing President.

Felix Frankfurter [15]

Brandeis' Letter to Balfour, November 26, 1918

My dear Mr. Balfour:
I venture to introduce Dr. Stephen S. Wise of New York, who at my request, goes to London and Paris as head of our Zionist delegation and as my personal representative.[16]

14. Ibid. (Reel 4)
15. Ibid. (Reel 4)
16. Ibid. (Reel 4)

44

Cable

December 2, 1918

Chiam Weizmann
London, England

Cable twenty-nine received. Wise and others sail this week. Hope Frankfurter will follow soon.

Louis D. Brandeis [17]

In a letter to Dr. Schmarya Levin, dated December 4, 1918, Justice Brandeis writes: "I shall not say goodbye, as you promised we should meet again soon; but I cannot let you sail without saying once more, how much the Jews of America and I in particular, are indebted to you." [18]

In a letter to Jacob R. Werlin, Houston, Texas, dated February 17, 1919, Brandeis writes: "Let me thank you for yours of the 12th with valued enclosures on Zionism. Our immediate tasks are to enroll as members substantially every Jew in America. From you we ask unremitting effort until every Jew in Texas joins the organization.

"I trust that you will report from time to time to the New York office the progress you are making." [19]

Paris, October 14, 1919

My dear Mr. Brandeis:

I regret not to have had the pleasure of seeing you on your way to New York. I hope that you have had a good journey and that you are satisfied with your stay in Palestine.

. . . You ask me to contribute a sum of 12,000 pounds

17. Ibid. (Reel 3)
18. Ibid. (Reel 3)
19. Ibid. (Reel 4)

towards the total outlay of 24,000 pounds required to organize the service which you wish to see established. I hold the said sum of 12,000 pounds at your disposal and ask you merely to be kind enough to let me know your plans, as I have studied the question for a long time and my experience may help to carry them out.

. . . I shall be very happy, my dear Mr. Brandeis, to work with you and to seek in every way to further the development of Palestine.

Believe me to remain,

Sincerely yours,
Edmond de Rothschild [20]

The following event will clearly illustrate that nothing harmful to the movement would ever escape Brandeis' attention:

The Henry Morgenthau Mission was something he suggested for himself. Early in June, 1917, he departed for Egypt, and from here, using his former connections as Ambassador to Turkey, he was supposed to get an invitation from the Turks to go to Palestine for the purpose of helping the Jews. The real purpose, however, was to make a separate peace with Turkey, separating her from her Allies, the Central Powers.

Felix Frankfurter was amazed when he was notified that he was to join the Morgenthau Mission.

. . . I suppose there never was a more fantastic mission on which I found myself sent, or included, than the so-called Morgenthau Mission in June and July, 1917.

. . . I was then an assistant to the Secretary of War.

. . . I didn't want to go. I had other things I wanted to do in connection with the War. Then one fine day I had a letter from the President saying, 'I learn with much satisfaction that you've agreed to go with Ambassador Morgenthau.' [21]

20. De Haas Papers (Reel 5)
21. *Felix Frankfurter Reminisces* (p. 145-46)

The following quotation is from an article by William Yale. Captain Yale was Technical Advisor to the American Section of the International Commission on Mandates to Turkey: ". . . Justice Brandeis may also have suggested that Mr. Felix Frankfurter should accompany Mr. Morgenthau to see that the former Ambassador did not do anything that would run counter to the plans of the Zionist leaders in the United States and Great Britain." [22]

22. "Ambassador Henry Morgenthau's Special Mission of 1917" *World Politics; A Quarterly Journal of International Relations*, Vol. 1, No. 3, April 1949

Chapter 5

PRESIDENT WILSON AND JUSTICE BRANDEIS; FIRST WEEKS IN THE WHITE HOUSE

". . . His determination to use the great abilities of Louis D. Brandeis was indomitably persistent. He wanted him in his Cabinet, but the forces of opposition were too strong. He sought his advice privately on some of the great problems of the time; he wanted him as chairman of the Commission on Industrial Relations . . ."

In a letter to Brandeis, dated April 24, 1913, Wilson writes: "There is no one in the United States who could preside over and direct such an inquiry so well as you could, and I wonder if it is possible for you to strengthen the whole thing by assuming direction of it. It would gratify me very deeply if you could." [1]

In 1915 the United States Commission on Industrial Relations was in session in New York City, inquiring into the causes of industrial unrest. It was in that same year that President Wilson, to whom Justice Brandeis was friend and counselor, said: "A talk with Brandeis always sweeps the cobwebs out of your mind . . ." [2]

". . . After he became President, and even before, Wilson had sought the counsel of Brandeis on trust legislation, currency and labor problems. In spite of bitter opposition he had wanted him for his Attorney General in 1913, before McReynolds was appointed." [3]

1. *Woodrow Wilson—Life & Letters*, Ray Stannard Baker, Vol. IV (p. 36)
2. "An Estimate," Frank P. Wald, *Jewish Frontier*, Nov. 1936
3. *Woodrow Wilson—Life & Letters*, Ray Stannard Baker, Vol. VI (p. 114)

Sunday, December 9, 1917

". . . There had been some pressure upon the President to make McAdoo Director General if the railroads were taken over, but the recent talk of a 'prince imperial' in the administration may have reached his ears; at any rate, he was not at first in favor of the appointment. Tumulty urged him to summon Justice Brandeis to discuss the situation, knowing that Brandeis favored McAdoo, but the President would not do it. At five o'clock, however, he went himself on foot to Stoneleigh Court, where the Justice lived, appearing at the door quite unannounced. 'I could not request you to come to me,' he said, 'and I have therefore come to you to ask your advice.' " [4]

". . . Wilson often wished the concept of his counsel in matters on which he was an authority. Not once, but a number of times discussing humanitarian or progressive policies, he would say to me: 'I wish you would go to see our friend Brandeis, acquaint him with the problem and get his reaction.' Brandeis knew he was talking to the President through me, but I learned much in the conversations which often took a wide range." [5]

Wilson's opinion about Brandeis is very clearly expressed in his letter, dated May 5, 1916, to Senator C. A. Culberson, Chairman of the Committee on the Judiciary, explaining why he appointed him to the Supreme Court:

". . . I have known him. I have tested him by seeking his advice upon some of the most difficult and perplexing public questions about which it was necessary for me to form a judgment. I have dealt with him in matters where nice questions of honor and fair play, as well as large questions of justice and the public benefit, were involved. In every matter in which I have made test of his judgment and point of view, I have received from him counsel singularly enlightening, singularly clear-sighted and judicial, and, above all, full of moral stimulation.

4. Ibid. Vol. VII (p. 401)
5. *The Wilson Era—Years of Peace,* 1910-1917, Josephus Daniels, Sec'y of the Navy, 1913-1921 (p. 548)

49

. . . Of his extraordinary ability as a lawyer no man who is competent to judge can speak with anything but the highest admiration. You will remember that in the opinion of the late Chief Justice Fuller he was the ablest man who ever appeared before the Supreme Court of the United States. "He is also," the Chief Justice added, "absolutely fearless in the discharge of his duties." [6]

It is quite clear why Wilson was so anxious to have Brandeis as the Attorney General, and it was Colonel House who succeeded in eliminating him.

Colonel House was the President's most intimate collaborator; always at the President's side, coordinating, evaluating, and recommending. Although not a member of the Cabinet, he was often referred to in the press as "Assistant President House," or "The President's Silent Partner."

According to Lloyd George, ". . . Secretary Lansing was a mere cipher—an amiable lawyer of good standing and of respectable abilities, but of no particular distinction or definite personality. He just did what he was told and was never told to do very much . . ."

". . . House was about the only man that Wilson really trusted among his associates and counselors. He gave him that abnormal measure of confidence because House very adroitly gave Wilson the impression that the advice he gave was not his own but Wilson's idea . . ." [7]

House was not only bitterly anti-Zionist, but also deeply anti-Semitic.

In a letter to the President-Elect, dated New York, November 22, 1912, House writes:

> . . . I lunched with Mr. Brandeis yesterday. His mind and mine are in accord concerning most of the questions that are now to the fore. He is more than a lawyer; he

6. *The Public Papers of Woodrow Wilson*, Edited by Ray S. Baker & Wm. E. Dodd, Vol. II (p. 160-64)
7. *Memoirs of the Peace Conference*, David Lloyd George, Vol. I (p. 156)

is a publicist and has an unusual facility for lucid expressions . . .

. . . A large number of reputable people distrust him, but I doubt whether the distrust is well founded, and it would perhaps attach itself to any man who held his advanced views.

Norman Hapgood [8] lunched with us and I found in him an enthusiastic admirer of Brandeis . . .[9]

After this expression of opinion it is quite evident that House opposed Brandeis as a Member of the Cabinet only because he was Jewish.

In his diary, dated November 16, 1912, Colonel House relates: ". . . We (the President and House) talked again of James C. McReynolds as Attorney General. We practically eliminated Brandeis for this position because he was not thought to be entirely above suspicion and it would not do to put him in such a place." [10]

In his diary of December 18, 1912, House related: ". . . We discussed again the Attorney General-ship and he asked about Brandeis. I told him that it was with much regret that I had to advise against him, that I liked him personally but he was not fit for that place." [11]

In his diary of January 17, 1913, House relates: ". . . We discussed the Attorney General-ship and we practically eliminated Brandeis from any Cabinet place. It was my opinion that it would be unwise to put him in." [12]

In his diary of January 24, 1913, House relates: ". . . We had dinner together quietly and enjoyably. I did not permit the telephone to be connected.

"We talked of Brandeis and the Governor suggested him for Solicitor General. I told him again that it would not be

8. Editor of *Collier's Weekly* & later of *Harper's Weekly*
9. *Intimate Papers of Colonel House*, Charles Seymour (p. 91)
10. Unpublished Diaries of Colonel House, Vol. I (p. 21) (Yale University Library)
11. Ibid. (p. 35)
12. Ibid. (p. 71)

wise to appoint him to anything of a legal nature, and in this view I think he finally concurs." [13]

In his diary of March 5, 1915, House relates: ". . . Sir Edgar Spayer called at ten this morning. He is the most sorrowful little Jew I have met in a long time." [14]

In his diary of October 12, 1916, House relates: "The day started briskly. Bernard Baruch rang me up to say he was sorry the President had appointed him on the Council of National Defense. I doubt his sorrow as much as I doubt the wisdom of the President's making the appointment. He might have chosen a more representative businessman. As it is, it places two Jews on the Council." [15]

In his diary of May 27, 1917, House relates:

". . . Vance McCormick telephoned from Harrisburg very much concerned about the proposed appointment of Bernard Baruch as purchasing agent for the United States and the Allies. He will have an expenditure of nearly a billion a week, and McCormick agrees with me that he is not the type of man the President should appoint. I believe Baruch is able and I believe he is honest, but I do not believe the country will take kindly to having a Hebrew Wall Street speculator given so much power. He is not the type that inspires confidence.[16]

In his diary of May 28, 1917, House continues on the same subject: ". . . I telephoned Vance McCormick advising him not to make too much of a protest against Baruch, for I think the President's mind is practically closed." [17]

In a letter, dated September 20, 1917, Colonel House writes to the President:

Dear Governor:
Thank you for your letter of yesterday enclosing

13. Ibid. (p. 84)
14. Ibid. Vol. VI (p. 66)
15. Ibid. Vol. IX p. 253)
16. Ibid. Vol. XI (p. 169)
17. Ibid. Vol. XI (p. 170)

Lansing's memorandum as to the preparatory work he thinks necessary for the peace conference . . .

I have the matter of organization pretty well outlined in my own mind subject to your approval. I think it will be necessary to have three men working closely with me here besides those studying special problems.

Among those here, I had thought tentatively of Mezes and Lippman—Mezes to be my confidential man and Lippman to be secretary. The objection to Lippman is that he is a Jew, but unlike other Jews, he is a silent one . . ." [18]

The confirmation of Brandeis' appointment as Supreme Court Justice was voted on June 1, 1916. President Wilson was greatly pleased.

In a letter to Morgenthau, June 5, 1916, he expressed his joy: "I never signed any commission with such satisfaction."

And on June 7th he wrote exultantly to E. P. Davies: "I am going to see the new Justice today and tell him how happy it makes me to see him on the Great Court." [19]

18. Correspondence: House to Wilson, Yale University Library
19. *Woodrow Wilson—Life & Letters,* Vol. VI, Ray Stannard Baker (p. 116)

Chapter 6

BRANDEIS AND THE BALFOUR DECLARATION

The first one to initiate the movement in favor of what was later called the Balfour Declaration was Sir Herbert Samuel.

". . . Already in November 1914, Herbert Samuel carried on discussions with Sr. Edway Grey, at that time Minister for Foreign Affairs, and with Lloyd George about the fate of "Eretz Yisroel" (the land of Israel), and made a strong appeal for a Jewish State. Grey's reply was that this idea has a strong sentimental attraction to him, and that he will promote it whenever an opportunity will present itself. Lloyd George also acquiesced.

In January and in March 1915, Herbert Samuel distributed to a few members of the government a memorandum bearing the title "The Future of the Land of Israel." At the same time Edwin Montague, who was in 1916 Minister of Ammunition and later Secretary for India, vehemently opposed the Zionist movement.[1]

". . . The interest in Samuel's memorandum by Sir Mark Sykes and James Malcolm can be regarded as a prelude to the actual negotiations which started later with the government. When Sir Mark Sykes, who was an Assistant Secretary in the War Cabinet, read Samuel's memorandum, he immediately went to his friend Dr. Gaster to discuss the matter with him. He was very

1. "From the English 'Chibat Zion' (The Love of Zion) Movement up to the Balfour Declaration," Joseph Frankel. *Yivo Bleter, Journal of the Yivo Institute for Jewish Research,* Vol. XLIII (p. 143-144)

54

much moved by the Zionist idea in which he envisaged a romantic mission. In October 1916, Sykes met with Malcolm, the President of the Armenian National Committee. Malcolm called Sykes' attention to the influence of the Zionists in America and the role of Louis D. Brandeis . . ." [2]

In the memoirs of Prime Minister Asquith, dated January 28, 1915, he writes: "I have just received from Herbert Samuel a memorandum headed 'The Future of Palestine.' He goes on to argue, at considerable length and with some vehemence, in favor of the British annexation of Palestine, a country the size of Wales, much of it barren mountain and part of it waterless. He thinks we might plant in this not very promising territory about three or four million European Jews, and this would have a good effect upon those who are left behind. It reads almost like a new edition of Tancred brought up to date. I confess I am not attracted by this proposed addition to our responsibilities, but it is a curious illustration of Dizzy's favorite maxim that 'race is everything' to find this almost lyrical outburst proceeding from the well-ordered and methodical brain of H.S." [3] (Herbert Samuel at the outbreak of the World War was a Minister in the government of Herbert Asquith.)

Weizmann describes his first conversation with Samuel on the 10th of December, 1914:

". . . Mr. Samuel remarked that he was not a stranger to Zionist ideas; he had been following them up a little of late years, and although he had never publicly mentioned it, he took a considerable interest in the question. Since Turkey had entered the war he had given the problem much thought and consideration and he thought that realization of the Zionist dream was possible. He believed that my demands were too modest . . . [4]

2. Ibid. (p. 144-45)
3. *Grooves of Change, A Book of Memoirs*, Rt. Hon. Viscount Samuel (p. 174-5)
4. *The Balfour Declaration*, Leonard Stein (p. 173)

"... When Dr. Weizmann on the advice of the famous editor of the *Manchester Guardian*, C. P. Scott, who had been converted by him to ardent support of the cause, visited Lloyd George in order to win his support for the Zionist ideal, he was told to get in touch first with Samuel . . ." [5]

"... Chaim Weizmann arrived in London in June 1904, with a tremendous enthusiasm for Zion. He immediately gained followers, but also opponents. His name was known in England through his utterances at the Zionist Congresses, and mainly through his opposition to Herzl. His main interest at that time was the establishment of a Hebrew University in Jerusalem. He remained in London for only a short time before leaving for Manchester. While in England he joined the "Chovevei Zion" ("Chovevei Zion" is the Hebrew name for the "Lovers of Zion," who were cultural, but not political Zionists). Herzl was very anxious to have the second Zionist Congress held in London, but since the Chovevei Zion were against it, it could not be realized. Later the situation changed. A great majority of the English Zionists became adherents of Herzl's political Zionism." [6]

Weizmann, as a chemist, was very successful in evolving a new method of producing aceton which was of great help to the British during the war. In 1916 he accepted the offer to serve as Director of the Admiralty Chemical Laboratories and London became the residence of the Weizmanns.

Weizmann's war service as a scientist made him known and had a great deal to do with the greater influence in pleading for the Jewish National Home.

"... It was Weizmann who brought to his aid the eager and active influence of Lord Milner, Lord Robert Cecil and General Smuts.[7]

5. *Mandate Memoirs*, Norman & Helen Bentwich p. 11-12)
6. *Yivo Bleter*, Vol. XLIII (p. 113-114)
7. *Memoirs of the Peace Conference*, Vol. II, David Lloyd George (p. 723)

"... At that time (no longer an opponent to political Zionism) the success of the Zionist Movement demanded that Weizmann become the President of the English Federation. His friends came to Joseph Cowen and appealed to him to withdraw his candidacy in favor of Weizmann, because Weizmann declared he would not run against Cowen (who represented the political Zionists). The noble Cowen not only withdrew his candidacy and promised cooperation, but also turned over two "anonymous" contributions of 500 pounds and 250 pounds for the Federation. Weizmann then, in February 1917, became the President of the Zionist Federation in England.[8]

Since Turkey entered the war, Great Britain, with her important strategic interests in the Middle East, was greatly concerned. Weizmann was a great believer that a Jewish Palestine under British protection would be good not only for the Jews but for Britain. However, while almost all the English government leaders turned to America with some glimmer of hope that aid might come from that quarter, Weizmann, probably due to sensitiveness about his citizenship, was reluctant to communicate with the Provisional Zionist Committee, since the United States was neutral at that time.

In a letter from Dr. Weizmann to Professor Kallen, dated January 24, 1915, he writes:

"The general attitude of the Provisional Committee as a body is not clear to me and I therefore must abstain from corresponding with them about Zionist matters, especially those which concern us as English Zionists ...

... Although I know your and Brandeis' personal attitudes and would be very glad to cooperate with you on Jewish matters, it seems to me that your views are not the predominant views of the Committee ...

... Since the arrival of Tchlenow and Sokolow in this country, it was their business to communicate with the Zionist Organization and not mine. I understand that they

8. *Yivo Bleter*, Vol. XLIII (p. 144-45)

did so and that they are in touch with Mr. Brandeis and the Provisional Committee and they are the responsible chiefs. They know all my work and I placed everything at their disposal. It is for them and not for me to move." [9]

The following is a letter to Weizmann dated July 29, 1915, signed by Benjamin Perlstein, Administrative Secretary and by H. M. Kallen:

"On several occasions our Committee has communicated with you but we have never received a reply from you directly. We learn, however, from Dr. Magnes, that you have written to him on a number of occasions, and that he has communicated with you frequently.

Dr. Magnes considers the exchange of correspondence as being personal, and is therefore reluctant to forward to our Committee, for our archives, copies, unless it meets with your approval. May I ask you therefore to send us copies of the correspondence from you to Dr. Magnes, eliminating, of course, references of a personal nature, or to advise Dr. Magnes that it meets with your wish that our Committee receive a transcript of the correspondence between you?" [10]

As I mentioned before the first one to initiate the movement in favor of what was later called the Balfour Declaration was Sir Herbert Samuel. There were two others:

The second was the Rt. Hon. Arthur James Balfour, the originator of the Balfour Declaration, the name of which survived even after the text of it was incorporated in 1922, in the Mandate of the League of Nations whereby Great Britain administered Palestine.

The first meeting between Balfour and Dr. Chaim Weizmann was a prelude to the Balfour Declaration of

9. *De Haas Papers* (Reel 7)
10. Ibid. (Reel 7)

1917. This was in 1906. Balfour was anxious to fathom the reasons of the Zionist attitude to the "Uganda offer." [11]

"He was told there was at that moment one of the younger leaders of the Zionist Movement, a Russian Jew Chaim Weizmann, by name, who had recently settled in England and held a post as lecturer in organic chemistry at the Victoria University. He asked one of his Jewish friends to arrange an interview with Weizmann who described to me (Blanche Dugdale) his conversation with Balfour."

". . . I began to sweat blood to make my meaning clear through my English. At the very end I made an effort. I had an idea. I said: Mr. Balfour, if you were offered Paris instead of London, would you take it? Would you take Paris instead of London? He looked surprised. He said: But London is our own. I said: Jerusalem was our own when London was a marsh! He said: That is true. I did not see him again until 1914." [12]

". . . On December 14, 1914, Dr. Weizmann had an appointment to see Balfour although Balfour was not as yet a member of Mr. Asquith's government. Dr. Weizmann approached him by advice of Professor Alexander of Manchester, himself a Jew acquainted with Balfour as a brother philosopher. Dr. Weizmann found the conversation of eight years previous to be still fresh in Balfour's memory.

". . . Mind you come again," said Mr. Balfour, "it is a great cause you are working for; I would like you to come again and again." [13]

. . . Balfour's interest in the Jews and their history was lifelong. It originated in the Old Testament training of his mother, and his Scottish upbringing. As he grew up, his intellectual admiration and sympathy for certain aspects

11. The "Uganda offer" was made by the British Government for a Jewish settlement in East Africa.
12. *Arthur James Balfour;* by his niece, Blanche E. Dugdale, Vol. I (p. 324-25)
13. Ibid. Vol. II (p. 163)

of Jewish philosophy and culture also grew, and the problem of the Jews in the modern world seemed to him of immense importance. He always talked eagerly on this, and I remember in childhood imbibing from him the idea that Christian religion and civilization owes to Judaism an immeasurable debt, shamefully ill repaid.[14]

In an address to a deputation of the Medical Unit, on July 14, 1918, the Rt. Hon. A. J. Balfour stated: "The destruction of Judea that occurred nineteen centuries ago is one of the great wrongs which the Allied powers are trying to redress." [15]

The third person was President Woodrow Wilson, without whose endorsement and approval the Balfour Declaration would never have come to be.

Already on December 6, 1911, then Governor of New Jersey, Wilson delivered at Carnegie Hall, New York, a stunning speech against the oppression of Jews in Russia. He started his speech by outlining the details of the treaty that existed between this country and Russia for some 80 years.

". . . For some forty years the obligations of this treaty have been disregarded by Russia in respect to our Jewish fellow-citizens. Our government has protested, but has never gone beyond protests . . .

. . . Here is a great body of our Jewish fellow-citizens from whom have sprung men of genius in every walk of life . . .

. . . Here is the final test of our ability to square our policies with our principles." [16]

Lloyd George wrote, ". . . President Wilson thus interpreted the Balfour Declaration in his explanation to the American public: I am persuaded that the Allied nations, with the fullest concurrence of our government and our people are agreed that

14. Ibid. Vol. I (p. 324)
15. *History of Zionism*, N. Sokolow, Vol. II (p. 131)
16. *The Public Papers of Woodrow Wilson*, Edited by Ray Stannard Baker & Wm. E. Dodd, Vol. II (p. 318-21)

in Palestine shall be laid the foundation of a Jewish Commonwealth." [17]

Wilson was regarded as an avowed advocate of the self-determination of small nations. ". . . President Wilson declared on January 22, 1917, three months before he entered the war, that Poland ought to be 'unified, independent and autonomous.' " [18]

Since he met Louis Dembitz Brandeis, Wilson's sympathies for the Zionist organization received new impetus. On the question of Zionism he was opposed by all executives and advisers surrounding him. It was Brandeis who had to counteract it.

Harden Advises Berlin

Maximillian Harden [19] writes in a recent number of *Die Zukunft* of the taking of Jerusalem and of the British Declaration. He lays stress on the importance of the Declaration and of the sympathies of President Wilson. "By the selection of Mr. Justice Brandeis as the man of leading rank singled out for the peace negotiations, President Wilson has shown his intention to use the influence of his government in favor of Jewish rights." [20]

". . . It seems strange to say that the Germans were the first to realize the war value of the Jews of the dispersal.

. . . The German General Staff in 1916 urged the Turks to concede the demands of the Zionists in respect to Palestine. Fortunately, the Turks were too stupid to understand or too sluggish to move.[21]

. . . In fact in September, 1917, the German government was making very serious efforts to capture the Zionist Movement.[22]

17. *Memoirs of the Peace Conference*, D. Lloyd George, Vol. II (p. 734)

18. Ibid. (p. 630)

19. A well-known German writer who became a Christian at the age of 16.

20. *Maccabean*, May 1918

21. *Memoirs of the Peace Conference*, D. Lloyd George, Vol. II (p. 722)

22. Ibid. (p. 726)

. . . The Balfour Declaration represents the convinced policy of all parties in our country and also in America, but the launching of it in 1917, was due, as I have said, to propagandist reasons.

. . . For the Allies there were two permanent problems at that time. The first was that the Central Powers should be broken by blockade before our supplies of food and essential raw materials were cut off by sinking of our own ships. The other was that the war preparations in the United States should be speeded up to such an extent as to enable the Allies to be adequately reinforced in the critical campaign of 1918 by American troops. In the solution of these two problems, public opinion in Russia and America played a great part, and we had every reason at that time to believe that in both countries the friendliness or hostility of the Jewish race might make a considerable difference." [23]

After reading these memoirs one cannot but admire the foresight of L. D. Brandeis about the war value of the American Jews; and this foresight was the main reason he devoted so much time from the first day of his appearance as the Zionist leader in order to keep increasing membership of the Zionist organization and to strengthen the Zionist ranks.

And now let us see how Justice Louis D. Brandeis, the "Silent Zionist Leader" managed to achieve the issuance of the Balfour Declaration in its final text. The question of Palestine, and the part that Zionism might play in relation to it, had been before the English Cabinet more than a year before Lloyd George became Prime Minister.

Cablegram

April 16, 1917

Following for Lewin-Epstein, Zionists, New York

Method of sending relief not yet definitely decided upon.

23. Ibid. (p. 724)

Shall telegraph when everything quite clear. Declaration approved by Foreign Office, but not passed yet through Cabinet. Telegraph result Frankfurter interview.

Weizmann [24]

Report to J. De Haas and Felix Frankfurter, Sunday, May 6, 1917 [25]

Mr. Brandeis reported at 3:15 p.m. that at 2:15 p.m. he had an interview with the President lasting three quarters of an hour, in the course of which he explained to the President the general Zionist policy. The changes in American Jewish affairs, the Jewish national problem involved in Polish autonomy, and the difficulties involved in the settlement of the Zionist question in Palestine as between the French and English policy. The President assured him that he was entirely sympathetic to the aims of the Zionist Movement, and that he believed that the Zionist formula to establish a publicly assured, legally secured homeland for the Jewish people in Palestine, would meet the situation: that from the point of view of national problems generally, he approved and would support the recognition of the nationality; that he would, at the proper time, make a statement, but that he would first bear in mind the situation arising in France and would exercise his influence in that direction, and that only thereafter would he consider making public his views, and that his utterances under that head would be drafted by Mr. Brandeis.[26]

24. Zionist Movement (1916-1917)—Yale University Library
25. Reported, dictated by Jacob De Haas, Wednesday, May 9, 1917.
26. *De Haas Papers* (Reel 2)

Cable

May 9, 1917

Following for James de Rothschild, from Brandeis

Two cables and documents received. We approve your program and will do all we can to advance it. Not prudent for me to say anything now. Keep us advised.[27]

Lloyd George writes: "We made preparations for joint action if and when the moment should have arrived for America to come into conflict . . ."

"When the news came through of President Wilson's decision, I suggested to the Imperial War Cabinet the sending of a special mission to America . . . On the following day it was settled that Mr. Balfour, the Foreign Secretary, should be head of the Mission . . ." [28]

Early in June 1917, Balfour was home from America.

". . . The Foreign Secretary (Balfour) felt more assurance about his policy of supporting Zionism since his trip to the United States where his conversation with Justice Brandeis has convinced him that he would have the sympathetic support of President Wilson." [29]

Cablegram

July 26, 1917

Following for Judge Brandeis, Supreme Court,
Washington

Chaim and myself leaving for Paris on important business, staying Hotel Meurice.

Sokolow [30]

27. Zionist Movement, 1915-17, Yale University Library
28. *War Memoirs*, D. Lloyd George, Vol. III (p. 1675-77)
29. William Yale, *World Politics; Quarterly Journal of International Relations*, Vol. I, #3 (p. 318)
30. Zionist Movement, 1916-17, Yale University Library

Cablegram

August 16, 1917

Following for Judge Brandeis, Supreme Court, Washington

Sokolow wires satisfactory interview, Premier, Italy, full support promised. Your letter received. Please write fully through your State Department or our Embassy.

Weizmann [31]

Cablegram

August 16, 1917

Following for Professor Frankfurter, War Department, Washington

General opinion rather favourable. Initiation must come from America. Expecting to hear results your interview before deciding anything further.

Weizmann [32]

Cablegram

August 18, 1917

Following for De Haas, Zionists, New York

Telegraph what way can send money. Government permit here only to Egypt.

Weizmann [33]

31. Ibid.
32. Ibid.
33. Ibid.

Cablegram

August 28, 1917

Following for Dr. Weizmann from Professor Frankfurter

Interest aroused here but it must come as British proposal. Thought you would be an excellent personal agency once it reached the stage.

Frankfurter [34]

House to Wilson; Mongolia, Mass., September 4, 1917: "Lord Robert Cecil cables as follows: 'We are being pressed here for a declaration of sympathy with the Zionist movement and I should be very grateful if you felt able to ascertain unofficially if the President favours such a declaration.' " [35]

House to the President; Mongolia, Mass., September 7, 1917: "Have you made up your mind regarding what answer you will make to Cecil concerning the Zionist Movement? It seems to me that there are many dangers lurking in it and if I were the British I would be chary about going too definitely into that question." [36]

Cable

September 19, 1917

From Weizmann to Brandeis

Following text declaration has been approved by Foreign Office and Prime Minister and submitted to War Cabinet:

1) H. M. Government accepts the principle that Pal-

34. Ibid.
35. Ibid.
36. Ibid.

estine should be reconstituted as the national home of the Jewish people.

2) H. M. Government will use its best endeavors to secure the achievement of the object and will discuss the necessary methods and means with the Zionist Organization.'

May expect opposition from assimilationist quarters. Would greatly help if President Wilson and yourself would support text. Matter most urgent. Please telegraph.[37]

Cable

September 26, 1917

To Dr. Weizmann from Brandeis

From talks I have had with the President and from expressions of opinion given to closest advisors I feel I can answer you that he is in entire sympathy with declaration quoted in yours of the nineteenth as approved by Foreign Office and the Prime Minister. I of course heartily agree.

Brandeis [38]

Cable

September 26, 1917

To Dr. Weizmann from Brandeis

It would be wise of you to get French and Italians to inquire what attitude of President is on declaration re-

37. Correspondence: Weizmann to Brandeis, Yale University Library
38. Ibid.

67

ferred to in yours of the nineteenth. Please let me know steps taken by them.

Brandeis [39]

Private and Confidential

October 7, 1917

"My dear Mr. Brandeis:

First let me thank you for the kind letters which you sent me. I appreciate so very much the words of encouragement coming from you. I was particularly delighted to meet Frankfurter and discuss with him our Zionist question and many a problem became clearer and easier after those discussions and I share with you the belief that our work will be much more fruitful in the future.

I must not hide from you the truth however that we are passing now through a very difficult stage in our work; my telegrams which you have answered so kindly have indicated already to you that the negotiations have reached the final stage; the British Government is considering very carefully the text of a declaration in favor of the Zionist movement, you know the text, and our Jewish opponents have not been idle; in fact, in the last three months they have displayed an activity which would have done honor to a better cause than combatting the Zionist movement. They published a series of pamphlets which represent nothing but some old speeches made by the champions of assimilation and circulated and broadcast these pamphlets.

Apparently they have also gotten in touch with their American friends, and have organized themselves into a fairly powerful group which is at present throwing in the whole of its influence against us. They have found an excellent champion of their cause in the person of Mr. Edwin Montagu, who is a member of the government and

39. Ibid.

has certainly made use of his position to injure the Zionist cause as much as possible.

On Thursday last the declaration was discussed by the War Cabinet and it was decided to adjourn it again. As far as I can make out, Mr. Montagu pleaded very hard against the text of the declaration and it is not unlikely that the government will propose a modified text to us and of course I shall telegraph it to you as soon as I know it.

I was summoned before the War Cabinet to state the Zionist case but unfortunately owing to a misunderstanding and to the fact that I was given only about half an hour's notice I could not possibly reach the War Cabinet in time and not through my fault I missed this rather historic occasion, but I trust that it will come again in a fortnight or three weeks when I shall have an opportunity of stating the Zionist cause before the highest British Tribunal.

For that opportunity I should certainly like to have my hands strengthened by a strong expression of opinion coming on behalf of American Jewry and I think that you will see the importance of this unique occasion and you will do what you can to help us. I do not presume to indicate to you the best form in which it can be done, as you know better the means and ways how it can be achieved in America. I only submit to you the supreme importance of this cause and its urgency. I do not think there has ever been an occasion like this, that a private person should be summoned before the Cabinet; I shall certainly try to represent our case to the best of my ability, but I feel—how enormous my responsibility shall be.

Another point is of great importance, you may know that an exchange of telegrams took place between our Government and your President. I do not know what Colonel House replied on behalf of the President to the inquiry made from here, but I conclude from various indications that the President, although quite favorable in principle to a declaration, seems to think that the time has not yet arrived for such a declaration. We here all think that the time has come to secure such a declaration although we may yet refrain from making it public; we all feel the necessity of having our negotiations which have lasted over three years brought to a conclusion by obtaining a declaration from the British Government.

Such a document would be of enormous value at present and would enable us to make the necessary preparations in case an advance of the British army in Palestine does take place soon. We must be able to lean on something definite so that we may go to the Jewish people and tell them that we have not only great hopes but a binding pledge from a power able and willing to champion our cause.

I enclose herewith a copy of a letter which Lord Rothschild and myself have sent to Mr. Balfour last week on the eve of the War Cabinet discussion. I may say that both the Prime Minister and Mr. Balfour and other members of the Cabinet like General Smuts, Mr. Barnes, the representative of labor, and Lord Milner have advocated our cause very strongly, but of course, they are all perplexed and bewildered by the attitude of the so-called "influential Jews"; it is difficult for them to understand such a position and if this particular attitude of the Jewish assimilationists is not successful in ruining our cause, it may be successful in weakening it or in postponing again the decision, and this is why I so urgently desire you to lend us a helping hand just at this moment.

I have no doubt that the amended text of the declaration will be again submitted to the President and it would be most invaluable if the President would accept it without reservation and would recommend the granting of the declaration *now*.

Mr. Ginsburg has shown me your kind letter to him and I think he had answered it already. I intend to make no special appeal to you or to your collaborators, the facts outlined in this letter are, I think, sufficient testimony of the historical importance of the occasion.

Once more I beg you to accept my heartfelt thanks and very best wishes. I have no doubt we shall be successful in the end. We may soon meet and initiate the real constructive work which will lead to the realization of our great hopes.

With very kind regards,

Yours very sincerely,
Ch. Weizmann" [40]

Cablegram from Weizmann (received through British War Division) dated October 10, 1917:

Following for Judge Brandeis

The Cabinet after preliminary discussion suggested following amended formula: 'H. M. Government views with favour the establishment in Palestine of a national home for the Jewish race and will use its best endeavours to facilitate achievement of this object; it being clearly understood that nothing shall be done which may prejudice the civil and religious rights of the existing non-Jewish communities in Palestine, or the rights and political status enjoyed in any other country, by such Jews who are fully content with their existing nationality, and citizenship.'

Most likely I shall be asked to appear before the Cabinet when final discussion takes place in about a week. It is essential to have not only the President's approval of text, but his recommendation to grant this declaration without delay. Further, your support and enthusiastic message to us from American Zionists and also prominent non-Zionists most desirable at once. Assimilationists doing utmost to defeat us. Your support urgently needed. Everything strictly confidential.

Weizmann [41]

The above letters from Weizmann to Brandeis indicate that

40. *De Haas Papers* (Reel 2)
41. Ibid. (Reel 2)

Weizmann still did not know that in problems relating to Zionism President Wilson was represented by Brandeis and not by House.

Also, Weizmann was evidently so eager to have a declaration issued, that he did not pay too much attention to the wording of it. Brandeis, of course, did not agree with the formula mentioned in Weizmann's cable of October 10, 1917.

". . . Late in 1917 the final draft of the Balfour Declaration, favoring a Jewish national home in Palestine, was cabled from Whitehall to the White House for Wilson's approval. Wilson waited for Brandeis. The Declaration was proclaimed only after revisions by Wise and De Haas had been endorsed by their 'silent leader.' " [42]

The Balfour Declaration issued by the Foreign Office, on November 2, 1917, read as follows:

> His Majesty's Government views with favour the establishment in Palestine of a national home for the Jewish people, and will use their best endeavours to facilitate the achievement of this object, it being clearly understood that nothing shall be done which may prejudice the civil and religious rights of existing non-Jewish communities in Palestine, or the rights and political status enjoyed by Jews in any other country.

The only victory of the Government opponents and assimilationists was the victory of one word against another word: *a* national home instead of *the* national home.[43]

Wilson to House, October 13, 1917:

"My dear House:
I find in my pocket the memorandum you gave me about the Zionist Movement, I am afraid that I did not

42. *Brandeis—The Personal History of An American Ideal,* Alfred Lief (p. 278)
43. See the declaration formula in Weizmann's letter to Brandeis, Sept. 19, 1917.

say to you that I concurred in the formula suggested from the other side. I do, and would be obliged if you would let them know it." [44]

House to the President, October 16, 1917:

"I will let the British Government know that the formula they suggested to the Zionist Movement meets with your approval." [45]

At the time Wilson found in his pocket the memorandum House gave him there were already rumors of a break between them:

September 6, 1917

". . . The usual rumor of a break between the President and myself is in today's press." [46]

The real break came much later, but when it did come the President evidently felt so painfully disappointed that he refused to see him any more.

". . . When Wilson was stricken down and became a helpless paralytic, he refused to see Colonel House—once his most intimate friend—at his bedside. Although he lingered on for years and saw many of his old friends, Clemenceau and myself amongst them, House, he would never receive." [47]

44. Correspondence—Wilson to House, Yale University Library
45. Correspondence—House to Wilson, Yale University Library
46. Unpublished Diaries of Col. House, Vol. XI (p. 265) Yale University Library
47. *Memoirs of the Peace Conference,* D. Lloyd George, Vol. I (p. 159-60)

Chapter 7

BRANDEIS AND THE ZIONIST COMMISSION
TO PALESTINE

The Balfour Declaration which was greeted with great joy by the Jews throughout the world was actually only a general state-ment of principle. It was very far from being the end of the Zionist task, it was merely the beginning. And here again the "Silent Leader"—Justice Brandeis—played the most deciding role in the work to translate the Declaration into action.

The first move in that direction was the authorization by the British Government of the Zionist Commission to Pales-tine under the chairmanship of Dr. Weizmann. By the an-nouncement of Foreign Secretary Balfour the Commission was designed as the representative of the Zionist Organization and authorized to act in an advisory capacity to the British authori-ties in Palestine with respect to all Jewish affairs and all matters pertaining to the creation of a Jewish National Home.

The sending of the Weizmann Commission, later known as the Zionist Commission to Palestine, was the first official con-crete step in realization of the Balfour Declaration.

The Commission arrived in Egypt on March, 1918, and soon thereafter in Palestine.

The main functions entrusted to the Commission were as follows:

1) To form a link between the British authorities and the Jewish population in Palestine.

2) To coordinate the relief work in Palestine and to assist in the repatriation of exiled and evacuated persons and refugees.

3) To assist in restoring and developing the colonies and in organizing the Jewish population in general.

4) To assist the Jewish organizations and institutions in Palestine in resumption of their activities.

5) To help in establishing friendly relations with the Arabs.

6) To collect information and report upon the possibilities of the further development of the Jewish settlement of the country in general.

7) To inquire into the feasibility of the scheme of establishing a Hebrew University.

All these reconstruction aims depended greatly on point one—the link with the British authorities.

The British armies had then conquered Palestine, and the authorities were administering occupied territory.

But almost all of these authorities were categorically against the Zionist aspirations; some of them regarded the Balfour Declaration as a forgotten episode of the war.

In a memorandum by Dr. M. D. Eder, Acting Chairman of the Zionist Commission, he tells the following story:

"On Saturday, the 18th of January 1919, I met Sir Mark Sykes together with General Storrs in Sir Mark's room, in the house of the C/C General Allenby, in Haifa. I complained to them about the hostile attitude of some of the British officials in Palestine towards the Jews. I cited the fact of Liet. Col. Hubbard, the Governor in Jaffa, who expressed himself publicly to British officers in the Y.M.C.A. hotel in Jaffa, in the presence of two French officers (Lieut. Saphir and Lieut. Lumoz) to the following effect: "If the Arabs will massacre the Jews in Jaffa I will not do anything to protect them; I will stand at the window, looking on and laugh at them:" [1]

The American Zionist leader, Robert Szold, who was a member of the Zionist Commission when Dr. Friedenwald was its chairman, relates the following: ". . . Sir Ronald Storrs, Governor of the District of Jerusalem, knew of the Balfour Declaration, but he told me personally that he had had no

1. *The Friedenwald Papers* (Reel 30)

instructions to further establishment of the Jewish National Home. He said he could go either way—the way of the Arabs or the way of the Jews." [2]

". . . In his report of June 29, 1919, to the Actions Comité in London, Dr. Friedenwald recommended that practically every British official in Palestine be removed, as quickly as possible." [3]

The Weizmann Commission to Palestine, later called the Zionist commission, was, during the summer months of 1918, and later during the first few months only looked upon as an investigating body. After the Armistice, however, and especially when Dr. Friedenwald took over the leadership, it became a permanent going concern.

The following figures will show how deeply the Commission penetrated into the economic, educational and cultural life of the Jewish population in Palestine:

1) Loans—$39,686,402
2) Education & Culture Dept.—$41,724,846
3) Communal Organization—$1,036,066
4) Social & Economic Groups—$938,662
5) Agricultural & Colonization Dept.—$6,011,154
6) Public Works Dept.—$4,927,111
7) General Administration—$14,296,908
8) Administration Charges—$10,703,581 [4]

Brandeis' refusal to have American delegates participate in the Palestine Commission when they first left for Palestine, which had irritated Weizmann very much, was according to the opinion of some writers, due to the fact that the United States was not at war with Turkey.

This opinion seems to be groundless for the following reason: "On April 20, 1917, the United States severed diplomatic relations with Turkey. This was two weeks after the declaration of war against Germany." [5] Later, when the American Zionists

2. *A Galaxy of American Zionist Rishonim—Dr. Harry Friedenwald*, Robert Szold (p. 13-14)
3. Ibid. (p. 13)
4. *Maccabean*, August, 1919
5. *London Times Diary and Index of the War* (p. 330)

did participate in the Palestine Commission, there still was no war declaration against Turkey.

There seem to be two other reasons for this decision:

First: the interference by Colonel House. In a letter to Brandeis, dated January 11, 1918, Stephen S. Wise reports:

". . . I wish to take up with you briefly the matters which I considered together with Colonel House on Wednesday afternoon, with respect to the participation in the Commission. Colonel House felt very definitely that it was not wise . . .

. . . The Colonel seemed to feel very distinctly that we must not be involved in the matter. He put it very definitely: "In the first place, it is unwise, and in the next place it is not needed. Cable to Weizmann that you are ready to give all the money and counsel that may be needed. But the Government cannot give its sanction to any American participation in the enterprise just now . . ."

But the Colonel did add, as I presume De Haas told you: "I am not speaking for the President; I am deciding this question on my own authority alone . . ." [6]

Second: Brandeis must have been very anxious to establish more fully Weizmann's reaction to his ideas and principles. He was eager to assure that they become the objectives of the Commission. These principles finally led to the break between them.

In a letter to Weizmann, dated January 13, 1918, Brandeis writes:

"My dear Dr. Weizmann:

For reasons which Aaronson will fully explain, it is impossible for us to send anyone to join you on the Commission to Palestine or to confer with you in London before you leave. From my talks with Aaronson, I am convinced that you and your associates and the American Zionists are in perfect accord concerning the work before

6. *De Haas Papers* (Reel 3)

us; but I deem it advisable to repeat here one matter of fundamental importance.

The utmost vigilance should be exercised to prevent the acquisition by private persons of land, water rights or other national resources or any concessions for public utilities. These must all be secured for the whole Jewish people. In other ways, as well as this, the possibility of capitalistic exploitation must be guarded against. A high development of the Anglo-Palestine Company will doubtless prove one of the most effective means of protection. And the encouragement of all kinds of co-operative enterprise will be indispensable. Our pursuit must be primarily of agriculture in all its branches. The industries and commerce must be incidental merely—and such as may be required to insure independence and natural development.

I will take up with Frankfurter and Mack the framing of Charter provisions and regulations which may serve to advance these ends, and hope later to submit suggestions which you may find of value . . ." [6]

This letter was really the nucleus of the Brandeis Program which was six months later adopted by the Pittsburgh Convention, held in June, 1918, and the main points bearing on the Palestine policy read as follows:

1) All land, owned and controlled by the whole people should be leased on such conditions as will insure the fullest opportunity for development and continuity of possession.

2) The cooperative principle should be applied as far as feasible in the organization of all agricultural, industrial, commercial, and financial undertakings.

3) The fiscal policy shall be framed so as to protect the people from the evils of land speculation and from every other form of financial oppression.

Weizmann Reports to Brandeis, London, October 29, 1918:

"It is just three weeks since I have returned from Palestine. Things have been moving with such rapidity

6. *De Haas Papers* (Reel 3)

in the last month that I have felt quite bewildered, and in the first days, very disoriented. There were days when one thought that peace was quite at hand, and even present, one cannot help feeling that any moment may bring some dramatic development; it is therefore difficult to make one's plans.

My intention is, however, to reduce my stay here to a minimum and to proceed to Palestine as soon as ever possible, provided that the Peace Conference will not take place this winter. There were moments when we all here thought that it would be necessary for me to run over to the States. At this present time it is difficult to say whether the necessity for such a voyage exists. The situation, however, is changing with such rapidity, that events may, in the near future, compel me to go over to the States to discuss matters with you, so that a clear and definite policy may be worked out. May I briefly outline the position.

Politically there is no substantial advance made here towards the clarification of ideas about the National Home. I do not think that our statesmen have a very definite notion what one ought to do in order to advance the Cause. Everybody is very busy and very preoccupied with more urgent business, and the Zionist question in its political aspects is, for the time being, relegated to the background. Events in the East, however, are developing, and certain things are happening which, no doubt, may prejudice our future in Palestine unless immediate action is taken; and I trust that I am going to make my point clear. With the complete conquest of Palestine and Syria by General Allenby's armies, two new factors appear on the scene: 1) The Arab government in Damascus, and 2) The enforcing of the Sykes Picot Agreement.

Both these facts are of fundamental importance for our future and we ought to be quite clear about their meaning. The establishment of an Arab government in Damascus and in certain parts of the north of Syria may be of great benefit to us if we continue to carry out the policy as laid down in the conversation with Ameer

79

Feisal during my visit to his headquarters last summer. Aaronson [7] will have reported to you about it fully, and I shall only recapitulate this subject very briefly.

An intimate cooperation between the Arab Government and the Zionist Organization to be established on the basis that Palestine is a Jewish sphere of influence (with boundaries still to be determined) and development. The Zionists to assist in the development of the New Arab States by supplying technical, political and financial advisors. It is obvious that such an agreement would lead to a consolidation of the near Eastern policy on a proper and natural basis, and it would be left to the two races interested in the Near East to settle ultimately their own destiny without very much interference from the outside. But obviously this natural state of things is vitiated by the diplomatic agreement to which I have already referred. The exact text of the Sykes Picot Agreement is still unknown to the world: fragments of it have been published by the Bolsheviks and also recently by the French press. Tsarist Russia was also a party to this agreement which is at present being enforced in Syria. As far as I can make out this agreement provides for a sort of mixed regime (almost international) for the country to the south of the line Akka-Safed. This agreement was made in 1916. The authors of it at that time did not take Zionist aspirations into account at all. It was kept a strict secret. I got to know about it on April 23rd and then saw Lord Robert Cecil about it.

The entry of America into the war and the Russian revolution, completely changed the position as pointed out both in my interview with Lord Robert Cecil and my letter to Mr. Balfour, but, nevertheless, the agreement is still treated as a reality, and although everybody here and also in Palestine agrees that it is a flagrant con-

7. Aaron Aaronson was the discoverer of wild wheat. He arrived from Palestine in 1912 in order to develop an interest in dry farming. He was considered one of the world's most notable agricultural experts. Brandeis regarded him as, "one of the most interesting, brilliant and remarkable men I have ever met with." (*Maccabean*, June, 1919)

tradiction to the principle of self-determination, the agree
ment is treated as a *fait accompli* for the time being, not
subjects to revisions. This has already led to a very considerable amount of trouble in Syria, and it certainly
prejudices our own affair very seriously.

I thought it my duty to draw your attention to a
grave situation which I am sure can be remedied only
with the help of our friends in America. Whether,
after you have received this letter, you think it essential
that I should come over for a short and unofficial visit
to America or not, I must leave to your good judgment,
but I feel strongly that the situation requires dealing with
without delay. Of course, the difficulties of the whole
position are the exaggerated claims of the French on
Syria. These claims do not take into account either
Jewish interests in Palestine, or Arab interests in Syria.
Therefore, it is the duty of the Jews at present to defend
their interests vigorously, and I hope that America would
support them. I shall probably have an opportunity of
seeing the Prime Minister soon, and putting before him
the whole situation.

Sir Mark Sykes is leaving for Palestine and Syria
soon; he has left today, only for a very short time, I
understand.

I enclose copy of two letters which I have written
to Mr. Balfour from Palestine, and also a record of my
interview with Lord Robert Cecil to which I have
referred.

(The letter also refers to the need for more financial
help.)

. . . I respectfully draw your attention to this, as
without sufficient funds our work and activity here and
in Palestine must seriously suffer.

> With kindest regards,
> I remain yours very sincerely,
> Ch. Weizmann [8]

8. *De Haas Papers* (Reel 3)

81

British Delegation, Paris
February 20, 1919

Dear Dr. Weizmann:

I have been thinking over very carefully our recent conversation and the general situation in Palestine, both as it exists now and will exist as soon as peace is signed. It seems to me that upon you, as Zionist leader, falls a very great responsibility at this moment, not only to your own people, but to the British Government and to the future of Palestine as a country in which the main object must be the establishment of peaceful, prosperous and happy conditions, not merely for the Jews who go there but for the whole of the population that has been oppressed and ground down for centuries.

It would be idle to deny that at present Zionism is unpopular in Palestine and that much of the odium falls and will fall not so much upon the Zionists and yourself as upon the British. Do not make Britain's task of facilitating the development of the National Home more difficult than the inherent difficulty of the task is at present.

Let me be perfectly frank with you. I do not like such phrases as "Jewish Commonwealth" and "Jewish Palestine." They excite fears and opposition, and Palestine will always be a "House of prayer for many nations." I hold so very strongly that "political" Zionism can but embarrass the British Government at present that I do urge you to do what you can as a statesman to resist the tendency which I note in the *Jewish Chronicle* to prophesy smoother things and gain the plaudits of people who do not know the actual conditions in Palestine, and are anxious for "panaceas." As a politician myself, I know how the pressure of constituents urges a political

82

leader or even speaker to say what will be popular rather than what is true statesmanship.

The time to talk of Jewish political prodominance in Palestine or of a Jewish State or Commonwealth (the two words mean really the same thing to 999 out of 1,000) or of a Jewish Palestine is not yet. It will only be the time for such a program when there exists in Palestine a far larger proportion of Jewish Palestinian citizens who have proved by their actions that their neighbors' present fears are groundless and that they have come to Palestine as self-dependent citizens to establish by precept and example a life and civilization of justice and progress worthy of the highest and noblest ideals of Deuteronomy and Isaiah.

May I as one who is really anxious for the true success of your movement urge you to exercise your great influence over the next week's congress to ensure moderation, patience, trust and practical resolution rather than to press forward political claims and to force the pace?

I believe you can trust the British people and the future British Government to behave honourable and justly, and that it is not necessary to secure a political position, which may, to my mind, embarrass both you and us in practical work in evolving the better Palestine.

I have been going carefully through the scheme and I am still uneasy about the proposed Constitution and functions of the Jewish Council for Palestine. I don't like political or extra-Palestinian popular control of such a body. I want to see it perform effectively the gigantic task of agricultural and industrial development, or organizing immigration and colonization as a great non-profit making public utility without the addition of political functions. I would put education under a separate body and I would on no account let it be the body which is to act as the liaison between the British administration and the Jewish citizens of Palestine, who, in my opinion, should have their own assembly.

I don't know what the opinion of the British Government is on the scheme you have put before the Peace Conference but they are not committed in any way, and I cannot, after full deliberation, feel that I personally can advise them if I am asked to accept the Jewish Council Scheme without very full consideration in detail.

Mr. Balfour told the Council of Ten on the 18th that he wanted the question of Zionism taken up shortly and asked that you should be heard. Hankey tells me that they will be ready to hear you any time, but that was before Clemenceau's wounding yesterday.

I assume that you will submit the names of three or four brief speakers who will support you. I do hope that they and you will put their case as completely and practically as is possible in a brief hour or so and in such a manner as to disarm criticism. The only opposition— I will not call it opposition—the only points on which I feel certain the Conference will want to be satisfied are:

1) That there is no proposal to subject the non-Jews of Palestine to the direct rule of the Jewish minority.

2) That the Christian and Moslem Holy Places (by the former I mean only; a. Church of the Nativity of Bethlehem, b. the Churches of Jerusalem, c. Nazareth) will be preserved in perpetuity to the possession, guardianship and administration of exclusively Christian and Moslem authorities appointed ad hoc.

3) That complete civil, political and religious equality for all citizens of Palestine shall be established both before the laws and in regard to government posts.

Given these three fundamentals, I see no reason why you should not press for such economic guarantees as will assure Jewish immigration and their provision of homes, subsistence, work, freedom of local and cultural development for the immigrants.

I know you would like me to accept some such phrase as "Jewish Commonwealth" but I honestly feel that such a phrase will be an embarrassment both to your future practical work and to the British administration.

84

I am a little nervous of your congress as it is clear that some of the delegates want to go farther and I only hope wisdom will guide them into paths of practical statesmanship based upon knowledge of existing Palestinian and Near Eastern conditions.

Excuse this long letter and please receive it in the spirit in which it is meant, *vide*, in the spirit of a well-wisher who is in a position to look at circumstances from the outside, who feels it his duty to express a word of caution to one who has great responsibilities before history and the world as a whole.

Yours very sincerely,
W. Ormsby Gore [9]

Ormsby-Gore's letter seemed to have reminded Weizmann of his Zionist activities as a "Chovev Zion" (a cultural Zionist) and as the focal point of that activity, his life-dream for a Hebrew University in Jerusalem.

The fifth meeting of the Advisory Committee to the Palestine Office was held at the residence of the Right Hon. Mr. Herbert Samuel, on May 10, 1919.

Present: The Right Hon. Mr. Herbert Samuel (in the chair); Dr. Weizmann; Dr. Jacobson; Messrs. James de Rothschild, Alfred Zimmern, J. Simon, J. Rosoff, B. Flexner, B. Cohen, Commander Hogarth, Major, the Hon. W. Ormsby-Gore, Mr. Toynbee, Lieut. Col. Gribbon and Mayor Money.

The discussion was mainly concentrated on the various problems in connection with the realization of the Balfour Declaration.

. . . The Chairman mentioned that it was necessary to get the economic and financial measures which the Committee wishes to take, prepared in advance so that if the Peace Conference decides along the lines proposed by

---

9. *De Haas Papers* (Reel 3)

the Zionist Organization, they should be ready to do their part and not to be unprepared . . ."[10]

Ormsby-Gore, concluding his speech said:

". . . Well, I have always urged Dr. Weizmann who will bear me out, to get as far as possible the political aims of Zionism in the background and concentrate on practical work and practical development. I am convinced that it is by practical development only that you will be able to counteract forces which are antagonistic, not only to you Zionists, but to us British, to establish peace and stability in the Near East as a whole. These are my general views as a whole." [11]

Weizmann told of his conversation with French leaders and expressed his opinion about Ormsby-Gore's statement to get as far as possible the political aims of Zionism in the background.

". . . They distinctly charged the British with an anti-French policy in Syria, the presence of French in Syria and the presence of British in Palestine would make for safety. That was more or less the trend of the remarks . . .

. . . At the Opera House meeting which took place in London, shortly after November 2, 1917, at which Major Ormsby-Gore was also present, Lord Robert Cecil said that he hopes that as an outcome of the war Turkey would be broken up and Arabia would go to the Arabs, Armenia to the Armenians and Judea to the Jews. It is quite natural that a statement like this made by a responsible member of the British Government should be interpreted by many that a Jewish State is going to be founded in Palestine. No responsible Zionist leader ever speaks of a Jewish State in Palestine now. I was, and am, constantly attacked by the Jewish press for being so moderate . . ." [12]

10. *Dr. Friedenwald Papers* (Reel 30)
11. Ibid. (Reel 30)
12. *Dr. Friedenwald Papers* (Reel 30)

Executive Committee Meeting, August 26, 1919, offices of Nathan Straus, Judge Mack in the chair.

"The chairman welcomed Dr. Friedenwald and Mr. Szold who had just returned from Palestine, where they had served as members of the Zionist Commission, and expressed the deep gratitude of the organization for the sacrifices they had made in leaving their dear ones, and for the magnificent work they had accomplished . . ." [13]

Report by Dr. Friedenwald:

". . . It is not necessary for me to tell you now what the difficulties were which we found on reaching Palestine. When Mr. Szold, Mr. Robinson and I came to Palestine, I think we can say that the work of the Commission was about as disorganized as it possibly could be. The entire work was resting upon the shoulders of one man who was ill—Mr. Lewin-Epstein. Commandant Bian Chini [14] took comparatively little part in the work at that time, but later on, I think, he took a very important part. Dr. Eder and all the other members of the Commission were away, and it was a very difficult thing to say how we should start the work . . .

. . . After our financial difficulties had passed, we went through another period of very great anxiety, on account of the Arab situation which was very threatening about the first of April. What gave us most concern was that the authorities did not seem to appreciate, as we thought, the seriousness of the situation . . .

. . . The work went on, insofar as the internal work of the Commission was concerned, very satisfactorily, but we felt that it was a great disadvantage to us to be in Jaffa. Every pressure possible was brought to bear upon us to remain there. The Committee which represents the various parties and groups in Palestine, the "Vaad Haz-

13. Ibid. (Reel 30)
14. Bian Chini, who was an ardent Zionist, represented the Jews in Italy.

mani," was very strongly in favor of our remaining in Jaffa. It was pointed out by some that it would cut us off from the new "Yishuv" if we left Jaffa . . .

. . . In spite of that we found it was necessary to go; that it was the only way. *

We could thus remain in touch with the British authorities and we so opened our main office in Jerusalem keeping a separate office in Jaffa, and we went to Jaffa every week or two and likewise had meetings there of the Commission . . .

. . . In consequence of the closer connection with the authorities we came into cordial relations with them. Nevertheless, in spite of the fact that our relations were so cordial and friendly, personally we felt that the Commission as a Commission was not able to carry through those things with the authorities which we had expected it to. We found exceedingly great difficulty (I take it that this is an Executive meeting and I will speak frankly and not for publication), with the fact that there was a lack of sympathy with all that our movement stood for, that the authorities, both high and low, had no interest in the work of the Commission, or in the purposes of the Commission, and had no intention nor had they any directions in forwarding or aiding its purposes. We were impressed, over and over again, with the statement that they are there simply to keep order, to keep the "status quo" and if the Peace Conference had any desire to hand over Palestine to the Commission, or make provisions for a Jewish Commonwealth, it was something for them to do later on; that the present military authorities have no interest whatsoever, and have no instructions. We heard this fact, that they had no instructions, from several of the higher officials, and they said it partly as an excuse, partly as an explanation of their attitude. If that would have been all, we probably would have gone on patiently

* The Commission's move to Jerusalem was also caused by the belief that when a Jewish State if finally established, Jerusalem should be its capital.

88

waiting for the time when the Mandate was given, but we felt convinced that there was a real undercurrent of hostilities in certain quarters. Later on, we found where that arose, in a measure. A great deal of it came from certain officials who stood very high in the administration, but it was very distinct, very hostile and one incident after another occurred which proved to us that it was not only a lack of sympathy but it was actual opposition, more or less hidden. It was not known to us how high this reached, whether the highest authorities of the land were also of the opinion that the Zionist idea was an impracticable one.

One thing became evident, that there was a growing fear on the part of the military authorities to anything favoring Zionism, out of fear of the Arabs. It was told us on several occasions that neither Great Britain nor any other power would hold Palestine for the Jews with the bayonet, and short of being at the point of the bayonet, it could not be held. I mention this, not because it is important in itself, but to make you understand the anxiety which they had caused us to feel.

We became impressed with the conviction that the very highest military authorities were opposed to the Zionist program, for one reason or another, and would use their influence against us, and we feared that this influence would make itself felt. It was that which gave us a greatest concern, and it was very difficult for us to convey that to Paris, and let me say, parenthetically, that one of the things which gave us the greatest concern was that we were unable, at all times, to communicate the anxiety we felt to those whom we thought ought to know them.

There was a time when we spent two days in meetings of the Commission to discuss whether Mr. Szold should go to Paris or not, to report on the conditions, and it was at the end of those two days of meetings that we determined that he should go, and everything was arranged for his going, when Bian Chini announced to us that he had determined to go to Rome and Paris, and we then changed our resolution about Mr. Szold's going, and decided that Commandant Bian Chini should convey the message, which of course he did. And even those messages, so we were told by letters, did not make the impression in Paris which we expected them to make. We were convinced that the danger was very great, because it seems that everyone who came to Palestine from without, excepting ourselves, came under the spell that it was an impossibility to carry out the Zionist program, and although I do not know what the American section is going to report, I am convinced that their report will be that it is a very doubtful program, or that it cannot be carried out now, because they came under that influence, and we feared, that that same influence might be conveyed to the people in Paris who were bound to us by all the ties that we believed would hold them, and yet we feared greatly.

When we heard that Mr. Brandeis was coming, it gave us the very greatest satisfaction, because we felt that we had in him a man who could make a just estimate of the whole situation, if we could lay it before him, and we were perfectly willing to submit to his judgment the whole matter.

I may say that the impression that was made upon us at first by Mr. Brandeis was that he thought we were very much more worried about the matter than we ought to be; that there was no real seriousness in the situation, and that we could rely thoroughly upon the British to carry out their plans . . .

But there was scarcely a day during his stay in Palestine that matters did not arise which brought up the various difficulties which we had. One thing after the other happened while he was there. For instance, there was a case where everything had been planned, every arrangement had been made so far as we know for a Jewish family to take over a certain hotel in Jaffa, and we were very glad for it would mean having a nice Jewish hotel there, and at the last moment when everything had been done, the arrangement was called off. Matters of that kind occurred during the time Mr. Brandeis was there, and he saw exactly as we had seen, that there was a serious danger in this attitude, and the greatest satisfaction which I have had during all the seven months which have passed since I have been away, has been in having brought on the part of the Commission to Mr. Brandeis' attention, the things as they were, to have had him see them as they were, and to have had him take steps, which he did take, and which he only could take to have them rectified." [15]

Due to the interference and influence of Justice Brandeis some of the top British authorities were called back and Colonel Minertzhagen, a pronounced pro-Zionist, was directed to Palestine. In a letter from London to Judge Mack dated August 8, 1919 Jacob De Haas relates the details of Brandeis' interference against the military authorities in Palestine.

"Practically by forced marching we reached London Tuesday evening, August 5th, all of us in good health and in good spirits. We found in Palestine that the complaints by Szold and Dr. Friedenwald, and previously by Lewin-Epstein, etc., etc., as to the general conduct of the administration were well justified, and therefore concluded that the remedy was not in the country nor with the G.H.Q. in Egypt, but in Paris and in London.

In Paris we met Sokolow and Felix, Gans, etc., but Weizmann was away in Switzerland and has not yet been seen. We hesitated for a day or so therefore, to go on with what we had proposed to do, but eventually on Monday, L.D.B. had a long session with Balfour and informed him on the facts. It was immediately apparent, as we had believed, that in the largest measures all the difficulties were due to separate administrative authorities,

15. *Dr. Friedenwald Papers* (Reel 30)

Palestine being under the Military and not under the Foreign Office. The government here was sincere and convinced as ever—one might say more so—on the whole line of operation. Indeed Mr. Balfour was quite angry at the Palestinian Administration, with the result that on Wednesday all the Administrative officials in Palestine were notified of the Government's attitude in a dispatch, copy of which is attached. This speedy action, following as it does the appointment of Colonel Minertzhagen to replace General Clayton in Palestine, gives us unbounded satisfaction. Storrs, I understand, is permanently out of the way and some other undesirable individuals are being removed. This will undoubtedly ease up the task for the acting members of the Commission now in Palestine.

The Chief has conferred with several British authorities and is seeing others tomorrow. He is going at the job with his characteristic straight-from-the-shoulder method. He was in Paris with the three American members of the Peace Delegation—Polk, White and Bliss, and enthused them. He has seen House, who stands pat, and while in the nature of things, nothing is final, they stand with us on the northern and eastern frontiers as do the British, who are reasonably open to discussion as to our desired southern extension.

We were asked to come here at a great rush because the Mandatory Commission was to get into action. However, the meeting of the Mandatory Commission is indefinitely postponed and none of us know just when it will meet. There is a suspicion that the whole talks will be transferred to Washington and I will cable you if we know anything.

So as to answer your letter about yourself and Flexner, the difficulty of the Mandate settlement is neither English, American or Jewish. The immediate policy that we are pursuing is to press for recognition of the organization as the authority in Palestine. If that is agreed to, as we hope it will be very shortly, then we will be able to face the inevitable delays with greater equanimity.

. . . The first job we see ahead is to clean up the country of malaria. This strikes our European friends as an unusual decision, but we conceive it to be all important." [16]

16. *De Haas Papers* (Reel 5)

Chapter 8

BRANDEIS AND THE KING-CRANE COMMISSION:
THE SECOND LANSING-HOUSE DEFEAT

After their defeat in connection with the Balfour Declaration, the King-Crane Commission was for the Secretary of State Lansing and for Colonel House, their last hope to damage the Zionist aspirations.

In a letter dated Paris, April 2, 1919, Lansing writes to the President: "In connection with the instructions which were agreed upon by you, Mr. Lloyd George, Mr. Clemenceau and Mr. Orlando on March 25, 1919, with regard to the sending of Commissioners from the Peace Confernece to make inquiries in certain portions of the Turkish Empire which are to be permanently separated from Turkey and put under the guidance of governments acting as mandatories for the League of Nations, I respectfully request your authorization to sign the appended letters addressed to Mr. H. C. King and Mr. Charles R. Crane, designating them as the two American Commissioners." [1]

In a letter dated Paris, April 15, 1919, the President replies to Lansing: "I have delayed replying to the enclosed because the other Powers involved seem to have virtually withdrawn from their agreement to send Commissioners to Syria, but in case we alone send them, these letters would be just as suitable, and I am very glad to authorize you to sign them." [2]

The President's letter makes it quite clear that the American Commission which is replacing the International Commission is going to investigate the situation in Syria.

In a letter dated April 14, 1919, addressed to the Hon. E.

1. *Papers Relating to the Foreign Relations*, Vol. XII (p. 747-48)
2. Ibid. (p. 748)

M. House, Hotel Grillon, Paris, Felix Frankfurter writes:

"On the assumption that the Syrian Commission is soon to leave for the East, I find it necessary to draw briefly to your attention:

1) In view of your assurance, and that of the President, which you were good enough to convey to me, the Zionist Organization feels secure that Palestine is outside the terms of reference of the Syrian Commission.

2) Agitation is now very rife from Damascus and Cairo. Therefore, the work of the Syrian Commission may have its influence in Palestine; and events in Palestine may, in their turn, bear on the field of the Commission's inquiry in Syria.

3) The Zionists are those interested in the work of the Syrian Commission, In our conversation you readily appreciated our duty to be watchful of Zionist interests in connection with the Syrian Commission, and you generously agreed that we should have the opportunity to cooperate with the Commission, though of course not as an official part of it.

4) In view of the intensified disturbance through the East I venture to suggest that authoritative contact with the Commission will be in the general interests of peace and not merely protective of the Zionist interest.

5) I hope you will therefore deem it appropriate for me to suggest that the American members of the Syrian Commission be asked to cooperate with the Zionist leaders during their work in the East. If it is agreeable to you the Zionist Organization will designate one or more representatives (to your liking of course), as unofficial liaison with the Commission.[3]

Of course, neither Lansing nor House waited for the report of the King-Crane Commission in order to make up their minds. They knew in advance what the conclusion of the Commission would be. As a matter of fact, House tried to make sure whether King was suitable timber for the Syrian mission.

3. *Brandeis Papers* (Reel 6)

". . . Among my notes I find one of December 20, 1918, that is one week after the American Commission landed in France, in which I recorded my thoughts concerning certain phrases or epigrams of the President which he had declared to be bases of peace, and which I considered to contain the seeds of future trouble. In regard to the asserted right of "self-determination" I wrote:

When the President talks of "self-determination" what unit has he in mind? Does he mean a race, a territorial area, or a community? Without a definite unit which is practical, application of this principle is dangerous to peace and stability.

Ten days later (December 30th) the fragment repetition of the phrase in the press by the members of certain groups and unofficial delegations, who were in Paris seeking to obtain hearings before the Conference, caused me to write the following:

The more I think about the President's declaration as to the right of "self-determination" the more convinced I am of the danger of putting such ideas into the minds of certain races. It is bound to be the basis of impossible demands on the Peace Conference and create trouble in many lands.

What effect will it have on the Irish, the Indians, the Egyptians, and the nationalists among the Boers? Will it not breed discontent, disorder, and rebellion? Will not the Mohammedans of Syria and Palestine and possibly of Morocco and Tripoli rely on it? How can it be harmonized with Zionism, to which the President is practically committed?

The phrase is simply loaded with dynamite. It will raise hopes which will never be realized. It will, I fear, cost thousands of lives. In the end it is bound to be discredited, to be called the dream of an idealist who failed to realize the danger until too late to check those who attempt to put the principle in force. What a calamity that the phrase was ever uttered! What a misery it will cause." [4]

In his diary of March 26, 1919, Colonel House writes: ". . . Felix Frankfurter was an excited afternoon caller. The Jews have it that the Inter-Allied Commission which is to be sent to Syria is about to cheat Jewry of Palestine. I assured him there was no such intention and gave him the real situation so he might take it to his fellow Hebrews.

I asked President King of Oberlin College to come. He has been at Coblentz doing some Y.M.C.A. work. I wanted to look him over and find whether he was suitable timber for the Syrian mission. The other man the President has decided upon is Charles R. Crane." [5]

In his diary of April 1, 1919, House writes: ". . . The President is becoming stubborn and angry, and he never was a good negotiator. So here you are. I think that the President is becoming unreasonable, which does not make for solutions. Nothing is being run in an orderly way. The Commission to Syria has been appointed and they are still awaiting instructions. There is no one to give the word, and so it is with innumberable other matters. It could be done so easily that it is maddening to see the days go by and nothing decided." [6]

In his diary of April 29, 1919, House writes: ". . . Frankfurter came again about his old trouble—'Palestine for the Jews.' He is afraid of the Syrian Commission. I advised him to go with them and keep in touch with the situation in that way." [7]

In his diary of May 24, 1919, House writes: ". . . Felix Frankfurter called to talk of the Jews of Palestine." [8]

The American Commissioners arrived in Jaffa, June 10,

4. *The Peace Negotiations, A Personal Narrative*, Robert Lansing (p. 86-87)
5. The Unpublished Diaries of Col. House, Yale University Library, Vol. XV (p. 113)
6. Ibid. (p. 127-28)
7. Ibid. (p. 180)
8. Ibid. (p. 215) Vol. XVI

1919. Ten days later, with unseeming haste, they had already taken their stand on Zionism:

The King-Crane Commission
to the Commission to Negotiate Peace

Jerusalem, June 20, 1919

For President Wilson

Probably at no time has race feeling been so sensitive as just now . . .

. . . Here older population both Moslem and Christian take united and most hostile attitude towards any extent of Jewish immigration or towards any effort to establish Jewish sovereignty over them. We doubt if any British government or American official here believes that it is possible to carry out Zionist programme except through support of large army. [9]

The final report of the Commission contains the following ideas and conclusions:

". . . No British officer, consulted by the Commissioners, believed that the Zionist programme could be carried out except by force of arms. The officers generally thought that a force of not less than fifty thousand soldiers would be required even to initiate the programme. [10]

. . . For the initial claim, often submitted by Zionist representatives, that they have a "right to Palestine based on an occupation of two thousand years ago" can hardly be seriously considered. [11]

. . . With a deep sense of sympathy for the Jewish cause, the Commissioners feel bound to recommend that only a greatly reduced Zionist programme be attempted

9. *U.S. Papers Relating to Foreign Relations*, Vol. XII (p. 769)
10. Ibid. Vol. II (p. 205)
11. Ibid.

by the Peace Conference, and even that, only gradually initiated. This would have to mean that Jewish immigrants should be definitely limited, and that the project for making Palestine distinctly a Jewish Commonwealth should be given up." [12]

The report of the King-Crane Commission came too late to be placed before the Peace Conference. President Wilson had returned to the United States. However, the President was so much against that report that he decided not to send it to the Peace Conference on Turkey.

This was a new blow by the President against Lansing and House, a blow for which the silent Zionist leader—Justice Brandeis—was in no little way responsible.

12. Ibid. (p. 215-16)

Chapter 9

BRANDEIS, THE SYKES-PICOT AGREEMENT AND THE PEACE CONFERENCE

The area of the Jewish National Home was not defined in the Balfour Declaration and the Sykes-Picot Agreement was the worst obstacle to overcome. It actually eliminated the implementation of the Balfour Declaration by the Peace Conference. And there again, Justice Brandeis, having the full confidence of President Wilson, was the deciding factor in this conflict.

The Partition of Turkey

"Secret Anglo-French-Italian Agreement of 1916-17, now made public divided up the Near East.

Turkey's entry into the war on the side of the Central Powers at once opened up the possibility of the partition of that country among the Allies in case the latter was victorious. This fact was formally recognized in Article IX of the Secret Treaty of London, negotiated with Italy on April 26, 1915. But it was not until early 1916 that Great Britain and France got together to arrange their differences in the Lavant and to divide the Sultan's domains between themselves in the event of victory. That they did make such a partition, and that all Turkey had been carved up and served out two or three years before the Peace Conference met has only recently become fully known to the world. The invitation to the United States to become involved in the Near Eastern situation by accepting a Mandate over Armenia takes on a new aspect in the light of the map and the agreements presented herewith.

100

The first result of the British and French decision to get together was the secret treaty known as the Sykes-Picot Agreement, drafted in February or March, 1916, and concluded on May 9th and 16th of that year. The text is as follows:

"The French and British Governments having acquired from information at their disposal the conviction that the Arab population of the Arab peninsula, as well as of the provinces of the Ottoman Empire, are strongly opposed to Turkish domination, and that it would be actually possible to establish an Arab State, or a confederation, both hostile to the Turkish government and favorable to the Entente powers, have opened negotiations and have examined the question in common. As a result of these discussions they have agreed upon the following principles:

1) France and Great Britain are prepared to accord recognition and protection to an Independent Arab State or a Confederation of Arab States in the Zones 'A' and 'B,' marked on the annexed map, under the suzerainty of an Arab chief. In the Zone 'A' France and in the Zone 'B' Great Britain shall have the right of priority in regard to enterprises and local loans. In the Zone 'A' France and in the Zone 'B' Great Britain shall have the exclusive right to provide advisors or foreign officials at the request of the Arab State or Confederation of Arab States.

2) in the blue zone France and in the red zone Great Britain shall be authorized to establish such administration, direct or indirect, or such control as they desire or they shall judge convenient to establish after agreement with the State or Confederation of Arab States . . .

. . . France and England therefore took the necessary steps a few months later to include Italy in the plan for the partition of Turkey in accordance with principles

101

already admitted in the pact of London. As a result the Sykes-Picot Agreement was supplemented by another equally secret agreement which assigned to Italy a broad zone in the south of Asia Minor and centering at Adalia . . .

. . . It is along the lines of these secret agreements that events have been moving Asia Minor ever since the wars; in fact, the sub-joined map throws a flood of clarifying light on the medley of annexationist activities in that region . . ." [1]

". . . The intention of the Allied Powers regarding the future of Palestine up to the end of 1916 are practically embodied in the Sykes-Picot Agreement. The country was to be mutilated and torn into sections. There would be no more Palestine. Canaan was to be drawn and quartered. But 1917 saw a complete change in the attitude of the nations towards this historic land.

. . . The carving knife of the Sykes-Picot Agreement was a crude hacking of a Holy Land. At the beginning of the war, Palestine was not in the picture. The mind of the Great Powers was on Belgium, Poland and Austria. The destiny of Palestine was left to the haggling of experts in the various foreign offices of the Allies." [2]

". . . Had a most disturbing telegram from Mack about Palestine boundaries . . .

. . . The thing is too big and (Chaim) Weizmann too little . . .

. . . Brandeis ought to go to Wilson at once and so I wired Mack." [3]

Great Britain admitted many secret commitments involving the fate of the Near East and its peoples. One of the most serious and perplexing problems to come before the Paris Conference

1. *Current History/A Monthly Magazine of the New York Times,* Vol. XI, Part III, 1920 (p. 499-505)
2. *Memoirs of the Peace Conference,* D. Lloyd George, Vol. II (p. 721)
3. *The Personal Letters of Stephen Wise* (p. 183)

of 1919 was that of the Near East, involving the disintegration of the Ottoman Empire.

The question of the boundaries of the British Mandate occupied a good deal of time of the Paris Peace Conference and Mr. Lloyd George relates:

". . . In agreement with M. Clemenceau it had been decided that Great Britain should hold Palestine. However, it had been recognized that the exact limits of the territories to be included in Palestine might be open to discussion, and on that account it had been proposed that any points in dispute, should be referred to an arbitrator to be appointed by the President of the United States of America. He (Lloyd George) felt sure the French representative would agree that the President would be very impartial in regard to any difference between France and Great Britain.

The French representative, Mr. Bartholet, in reply said: ". . . In regard to the proposal that President Wilson should be asked to arbitrate, should difference of opinion arise as to the territorial limits of Palestine, the French were unable to accept any such proposal, since President Wilson was entirely guided by Mr. Brandeis, who held very decided views." [4]

In his speech, Mr. Bartholet also said: ". . . That all the Jews in France are anti-Zionists, and had no desire at all to go to Palestine." [5]

". . . While the discussions were proceeding a telegram arrived from Justice Brandeis of the Supreme Court of Justice in Washington. It had been addressed to Dr. Weizmann and read as follows:

"16 Februaary, 1919. Please convey Prime Minister Lloyd George following message from myself and all those associated with me in the Zionist Organization of America —quote: My associates of the Zionist Organization of

4. *Memoirs of the Peace Conference*, D. Lloyd George, Vol. II (p. 758-60)
5. Ibid. (p. 765)

103

America cabled me from Paris that in Conference re Turkish Treaty France now insists upon terms of Sykes-Picot Agreement. If this contention of France should prevail it would defeat realization of promise of Jewish Home for Sykes-Picot Agreement divides country in complete disregard of historic boundaries and actual necessity rational northern and eastern boundaries indispensable to self-sustaining community and economic development of country. North Palestine must include Litany River watersheds of Hermon and East must include Plain Of Jaulan Hauran if Balfour Declaration subscribed to by France as well as other Allied and Associated Powers is to be made effective. These boundaries must be conceded to Palestine. Stop. Less than this would produce mutilation promised Home. Stop. Balfour Declaration was public promise proclaimed by your Government and subscribed to by Allied Powers. I venture to suggest that in your assuring just settlement boundaries Palestine Statesmen Christian Nations keep this solemn promise to Israel." [6]

". . . The Zionist Mission, representing the Zionist Organization and the Jewish population of Palestine, was received by the Supreme Council on February 27, 1919. Mr. Sokolow read the following extract from a memorandum which he had circulated.

. . . Point 3 (of this memorandum) stated: 'The sovereign possession of Palestine shall be vested in the League of Nations and the government entrusted to Great Britain as Mandatory of the League.'

. . . Point 5: 'The Mandate shall be subject also to the following special conditions:

'Palestine shall be placed under such political, administrative and economic conditions as will secure the establishment there of the Jewish National Home, and ultimately render possible the creation of an autonomous Commonwealth, it being clearly understood that nothing shall be done which may prejudice the civil and religious

6. Ibid. (p. 760-61)

104

rights of existing non-Jewish communities in Palestine, or the rights of or political status enjoyed by Jews in any other country.' [7]

". . . Later: Mr. Lansing asked Dr. Weizmann to clear up some confusion which existed in his mind as to the correct meaning of the words— 'Jewish National Home.' Did that mean an autonomous Jewish Government?

Dr. Weizmann replied in the negative. The Zionist Organization did not want an autonomous Jewish Government, but merely to establish in Palestine, under a Mandatory Power, an administration, not necessarily Jewish, which would render it possible to send into Palestine 70,000 to 80,000 Jews annually. The Organization would require to have permission at the same time, to build Jewish schools, where Hebrew would be taught, and to develop institutions of every kind. Thus it would build up gradually a nationality and so make Palestine as Jewish as America is American, or England is English. Later on, when the Jews formed the large majority they would be ripe to establish such a Government as would answer to the state of the development of the country and to their ideals." [8]

Among the various commissions set up by the Peace Conference was one to study the problems of securing equal rights for minorities.

". . . At the end of April 1919, a memorandum was put forward by the Economic Section of the British Delegation to the Peace Conference, in which it was suggested that some sort of guarantee should be exacted from the new states in reference to the interests of the transferred populations. The immediate case was that of Poland, a newly created State, which incorporated, besides a large number of Jews, other nationalities such as Germans,

7. Ibid. (p. 747)
8. Ibid. (p. 748)

Russians, etc. It was a delicate and complicated problem and one not to be settled in a hurry, and in order to give time for the working out of details, and as the Polish Treaty was to be signed at the same time as the German, namely, at the end of June, 1919, it was decided, in the case of Poland, to insert the following clause in the German Treaty:

'Poland accepts and agrees to embody in a Treaty with the principal Allied and Associated Powers such provisions as may be deemed necessary by the said Powers to protect the interests of the inhabitants of Poland who differ from the majority of the population in race, language, or religion . . .' [9]

Judge Mack and Louis Marshall were the heads of a commission which came from the United States to Paris in connection with securing equal rights for the Jews living in East European countries.

In his memoirs, dated June 26, 1918, Colonel House introduced David Miller: ". . . David Miller and I discussed at intervals, when I had time, matters relating to the Peace Inquiry, he having charge of the international law end of it." [10]

My Diary at the Conference of Paris

David Hunter Miller, Technical Adviser,
American Commission to Negotiate Peace

Tuesday, April 29, 1919

". . . I went over to see Col. House, and he agreed to see Judge Mack and Mr. Marshall tomorrow at 5 o'clock, and said it was quite all right for me to go away for a few days.[11]

9. Ibid. (p. 882)
10. Unpublished Diaries of Col. House, Yale University Library, Vol. XIII (p. 168)
11. Film 1-2, O.Z. 32, New York Public Library

Friday, May 2, 1919

. . . About 7 o'clock I stopped to see Col. House, who was talking with Wiseman [Sir William Wiseman was the head of the British Military Intelligence in the U.S.] about the League of Nations. I told him about the Committee appointment and what we were doing with the British. He said he did not want to offend the Poles as he thought more of the Poles than he did of the Jews, and I told him what I was proposing to put in, which he seemed to think was all right.[12]

Saturday, May 3, 1919

. . . Mr. Marshall came in and I told him that I did not feel at liberty to tell him what had happened at the meeting . . .

. . . The question of the rights of minorities was taken up and the sentiment was entirely against creating any communities such as the Jews want.

I saw Col. House in the afternoon and he thought I should not discuss with the Jews any details of what happened.[13]

Sunday, May 4, 1919

Judge Mack and Mr. Marshall came in and I told them I could not discuss the matter any further. They knew of the appointment of the Committee as they had learned it from Sir Herbert Samuel who had lunched with Lloyd George yesterday. I told them that Mr. Barthelot was the French member of the Committee and I advised them against attempting to see either Col. House or President Wilson.[14]

12. Ibid.
13. Ibid.
14. Ibid.

107

. . . I then went to the office and after a few minutes there went over to see Taussig with Hudson. I explained to Taussig my general view about the New States Commission and he and Hudson went to the meeting of the experts . . .

. . . Coming back from the meeting I stopped to see Col. House and told him of my talks with the Italians and also about the Polish matter. He remarked that Lloyd George had sold out to the Jews, to which I agreed.[15]

And now let us see again how the Silent Leader continues his Zionist work day by day, hour by hour.

Cablegram

Following for Justice Brandeis, Stoneleigh Court, Washington

November 29, 1918
Have received your message through Strauss. He informs me that you will probably accompany the President. Have received De Haas' telegram with names of delegates. Must appeal to you at this final and critical state to come over and if absolutely impossible to send Frankfurter. I understand how difficult it may be for you to travel, but we have reached the crucial point in Jewish history. It is our sacred duty to leave nothing to chance. Your presence here would render our position infinitely safe. Such is not only our opinion but generally admitted. Aaronson going to Paris. Am writing De Hass fully.

Weizmann [16]

15. Ibid.
16. Correspondence: Weizmann to Brandeis. Yale University Library

108

The following is a telegram from Brandeis, Washington, D. C. to De Haas, New York, dated December 27, 1918:

"Your telegram today received. Have also through Weizmann's office cable from Weizmann dated apparently December 22 as follows: In an interview today with Weizmann the Prime Minister declared that an immediate communication to President Wilson from yourself urging British Trusteeship over Jewish Palestine at this time would be of highest value. We consider the matter of British Trusteeship to be at a critical stage. The imperative necessity for such action by yourself was emphasized yesterday by Wise in an interview he had with Mr. Balfour. Stop. Felix and I doubt the advisability of my calling the President before we know the situation better as it will be disclosed at Wise's interview with House. And suggest sending in my name a cable to Wise immediately as follows. If you and Mack approve you know that I favor and have long advocated British Trusteeship under League of Nations for Jewish Palestine. Resolution of American Jewish Congress to this effect expresses the will and judgment of vast majority of American Jews . . .

I assume you will present these facts to the President and Col. House. It has seemed to us wiser that I should defer communicating directly to the President until you should have conferred with him or Col. House and advise me how matters stand. But I am of course ready to act immediately if in your judgment with full knowledge of the situation the exigency demands immediate action. Stop. Also cable Weizmann in my name that I have cabled Wise fully. Wire me what to do." [17]

17. *De Haas Papers* (Reel 3)

Telegram

From De Haas to Brandeis

December 29, 1918

Cabled Wise and Weizmann in accordance with your telegram after conference with Mack.[18]

In a letter to Hon. Arthur James Balfour, dated January 5, 1919, Brandeis writes: "I hope it will be possible for you to see Mr. Jacob De Haas, the British-born secretary of our Zionist Organization, who brings some suggestions in regard to Palestine, which seem to us of great importance." [19]

In a letter of the same date, Brandeis writes to Weizmann: "From Wise and others you know how much of America's advance in Zionism we owe to De Haas' devotion, knowledge and rare political experience and sagacity and how much I have leaned upon him throughout the four and a half years during which I have taken an active part in Zionist affairs.

De Haas will be able to give you my views on all questions which have already been presented for consideration, and as I have shared with him fully every thought on Zionist problems for years, will be able to present my point of view even on new matters; he will be able to do also to make clear to you America's possible contribution in men and money.

"I trust that Frankfurter will be able to sail next week." [20]

In a letter, dated January 16, 1919, to De Haas c/o London Zionist Bureau, his secretary, Blanche Jaboson, reports:

" . . . Today is just a week since you left for Europe . . .

" . . . Copies of all telegrams and communications of importance and interest are forwarded to Justice Brandeis daily . . ." [21]

Letter #2 from De Haas to Brandeis, dated January 29, 1919, the Carlton Hotel, London:

18. Ibid. (Reel 3)
19. Ibid. (Reel 5)
20. Ibid. (Reel 5)
21. Ibid. (Reel 5)

"At this writing Flexner and I have secured our visas and are preparing for our trip to Paris. Conditions here and the problems we are dealing with are somewhat in the order of events, as follows:

1) On January 21, Flexner and I had a long conversation with Weizmann, to which I believe I referred in my last letter and the outcome of which was apparently an appreciation of our position and the mutual understanding that we were not widely separated as to the policies to be pursued.

2) The next day we attended a meeting of the Political Committee. I spoke on the development and growth of the American organization and about the principles (Pittsburgh Platform) on which they stood.

Dr. Weizmann made a short answer saying that he shared our views on social justice." [22]

Cable

From Justice Brandeis through Admiral Sims to De Haas, Flexner:

February 10, 1919

Two cables received. Felix and Gans sailing on *Baltic* due to leave February 15th. Hope Flexner will remain in London to await their arrival.[23]

Telegram

From Felix Frankfurter to Justice Brandeis:

February 14, 1919

Would it not be well for you to send personal note through British Embassy to Mr. Balfour advising him I am

22. Ibid. (Reel 5)
23. Ibid. (Reel 5)

111

abroad on Zionist matters. Wire me at Harvard Club if you are writing.[24]

Representing the Zionists at the Peace Conference, Frankfurter appealed to President Wilson to endeavor before he leaves Paris to have the Balfour Declaration written into the Peace Treaty.

Wilson replied that Frankfurter has his permission to transmit the following statement to Lansing and the balance of the American Commission:

'I never dreamed that it was necessary to give you any renewed assurance of my adherence to the Balfour Declaration and so far I have found no one who is seriously opposing the purpose which it embodies . . .

. . . I see no ground for discouragement and every reason to hope that satisfactory guarantees can be secured.' [25]

Strictly Confidential: Memorandum of Interview in Mr. Balfour's apartment, 23 Rue Nitot, on Tuesday, June 24, 1919 at 4:45 p.m.

Present: Mr. Balfour, Mr. Justice Brandeis, Lord Eustace Percy and Mr. Frankfurter.

Mr. Balfour expressed great satisfaction that Justice Brandeis came to Europe. He said the Jewish problem of which the Palestine question is only a fragment but an essential part, is in his mind as perplexing a question as confronts the statesmenship of Europe. He is exceeding distressed by it and harassed by its difficulties. Mr. Balfour rehearsed summarily the pressure of Jews in Eastern Europe and said that the problem was, of course, complicated by the extraordinary phenomenon that Jews now are not only participating in revolutionary movements but are actually, to a large degree, leaders in such movements.

24. Ibid. (Reel 4)
25. General Records of the Dept. of State. Frankfurter to Lansing, May 23, 1919. *The Palestine Question in the Wilson Era*, Selig Adler (p. 324)

He stated that a well informed person told him only the other day that Lenin also on his mother's side was a Jew.

Justice Brandeis stated that he has every reason to believe that this is not so and that Lenin on both sides is an upper-class Russian. He continued to say that after all this is a minor matter, that all that Mr. Balfour said was quite so. He believes every Jew is potentially an intellectual and an idealist and the problem is one of direction of those qualities. He narrated his own approach to Zionism, that he came to it wholly as an American, for his whole life had been free from Jewish contacts or traditions. As an American he was confronted with the disposition of the vast numbers of Jews, particularly Russian Jews, that were pouring into the United States year by year. It was then that by chance a pamphlet on Zionism came his way and led him to the study of the Jewish problem and to the conviction that Zionism was the answer. The very same men, with the same qualities that are now enlisted in revolutionary movements would find, and in the United States do find, constructive channels for expression and make positive contributions to civilization.

Mr. Balfour interrupted to express his agreement, adding—'Of course these are the reasons that make you and me such ardent Zionists.'

The Justice continued that for the realization of the Zionist program three conditions were essential:

Firstly, that Palestine should be the Jewish Homeland and not merely that there be a Jewish homeland in Palestine. That, he assumed, is the commitment of the Balfour Declaration, and will of course be confirmed by the Peace Conference.

Secondly, there must be economic elbow room for a Jewish Palestine; self-sufficiency for a healthy social life. That meant adequate boundaries, not merely a small garden within Palestine. On the North that meant the control of water and be assured that Great Britain was urging the northern boundary necessary for the control of the waters. That was a question substantially between

England and France and of course must be determined by the Peace Conference. The southern and eastern boundaries, he assumed, raised internal British questions.

Mr. Balfour assented that that was the southern boundary but questioned as to the eastern boundary.

The Justice added that, of course, the interests of the Hedjaz were involved, but after all, the disposition of questions between the Arabs and the Zionists was, in effect, an internal British problem. He urged on the East the Trans-Jordan line for there the island is largely unoccupied and settlement could be made without conflict with the Arabs much more easily than in the more settled portions of the North.

Mr. Balfour pointed out that in the East there is the Hedjaz railroad which can rightly be called the Mohammedan railroad.

The Justice replied that there is land right to the railroad and Mr. Balfour stated that he thought that Feisel would agree to having an Eastern boundary of Palestine go up to the Hedjaz railroad.

Thirdly, the Justice urged that the future Jewish Palestine must have control of the land and the natural resources that are at the heart of a sound economic life. It was essential that the values which are being and will be created, because of the secession of Turkish rule and due to British occupation and Jewish settlement, should go to the State and not into private hands.

Mr. Balfour expressed entire agreement with the three conditions which the Justice hoped that while he was away at least nothing would be done which would embarrass the fulfillment of the three conditions which he laid down as essential to the realization of the Zionist program.

Mr. Balfour then stated that he understood Justice Brandeis' request that no decision be taken as to the boundaries and the extent of control over the land in any way counter to his view until his return in about four or five weeks. He thought it was perfectly safe to

114

give him the assurance that no decision will be taken on those matters during that time to embarrass the aims which the Justice indicated.

Mr. Balfour stated that he would be either in Paris or in London when the Justice returned and he hoped that he will report to him at once upon his return on the questions as they appear to him from a study on the spot . . .[26]

In a telegram from Jerusalem to the Zionists in New York, dated July 29, 1919, Dr. Friedenwald reports that: "Brandeis, De Haas, Friedenwald, Szold Party leave Jerusalem tonight for Paris." [27]

On September 9, 1919, Justice Brandeis reported to the National Executive Committee of the Zionist Organization:

"I will state the conclusions which I personally have reached from my visit to Palestine, and generally from conferences with our Zionists in Paris, London and elsewhere. I think that in large part, at least, the conclusions are shared in by others who were with us but I hope, Mr. Chairman, that you will ask the others specifically to state to what extent they may differ from any of the conclusions which I had stated, because while we have talked matters over much, I am not certain that they agree with everything that I say.

First, as to Palestine. The land: when you have seen it as we have, you understand how the love and the longing of the Jewish people has survived these eighteen hundred years. The beauty and character of the associations fully explain that. Again, the character of the land and its location make it possible that in addition to the present population, the country within the boundaries which we contemplate, developed agriculturally and industrially, as it should be, would give a home to six million Jews.

26. *De Haas Papers* (Reel 4)
27. Ibid. (Reel 4)

Second, as to the people: It is clear that Jews not only in eastern and southeastern Europe in large mass, but the Jews of the Orient and all parts of the world, in large numbers are again to go to Palestine, and immigration would be limited in speed and in numbers as far as the Jews are concerned, wholly by the ability of Palestine to receive them.[28]

Cable

From Brandeis to Balfour

February 1, 1920

We are deeply concerned at information that it is proposed to carry out the Sykes-Picot Treaty to mutilate historic Palestine and render all future developments impossible. Without Litany watersheds of Hermon Joulon and the Hauron we can accomplish nothing. We beg you to intercede with the British and French Governments. At this crisis your name has been associated with the promises which has kept our people alive during the two years of misery and anguish. I feel you will understand that deprivation of the natural boundaries of the country and the enforcement of the Sykes-Picot Treaty vitiate the promise and will spread an unforgettable woe among fourteen million people.[29]

Cable

From Brandeis to Andre Pierre Tardieu

February 2, 1920

American papers report your return to Cabinet. Am gratified you are in position to urge your colleagues in

28. Ibid. (Reel 4)
29. Ibid. (Reel 6)

the Government the importance of adherence on the part of the Government to the Balfour Declaration. That Declaration cannot be carried out without giving to Palestine as its northern boundary the Litany River and the watersheds of the Hermon and include the Plains of the Joulon and the Hauron. Public opinion in our country naturally depends upon you to urge these Zionist claims. I look forward to your quick reassuring word.[30]

Brandeis to President Wilson, Washington, February 4, 1920:

My dear Mr. President:
Negotiations in Paris on the Turkish settlement have reached so critical a state in their effect upon the realization of the Balfour Declaration for a Jewish Homeland in Palestine as to compel me to appeal to you.
My associates of the Zionist Organization cable me from Paris that in the conferences on the Turkish Treaty, France now insists upon the terms of the Sykes-Picot Agreement—one of the secret treaties made in 1916 before our entrance into the War. If this contention of the French should prevail, it would defeat full realization of the promise of the Jewish Homeland; for the Sykes-Picot Agreement divides the country in complete disregard of historic boundaries and their actual necessities. Rational northern and eastern boundaries are indispensable to a self-sustaining community and the economic development of the country. On the north, Palestine must include the plains of the Jordan and the Hauron. If the Balfour Declaration subscribed to by France as well as the other Allied and Associated Powers is to be made effective, these boundaries must be conceded to Palestine. Less than this would produce mutilation of the promised Homeland.
Neither in this country nor in Paris, has there been

30. Ibid. (Reel 7)

any opposition to the Zionist program. The Balfour Declaration which you made possible was a public promise. I venture to suggest that it may be given to you at this time to move the statesmen of Christian nations to keep this solemn promise to Israel. Your word to Miller and Lloyd George at this hour may be decisive.

Most respectfully and cordially,
Louis D. Brandeis [31]

Telegram

From Brandeis to Judge Mack, Zionist Organization, New York:

February 9, 1920

Saw Lansing this morning. He informs me he sent on Friday under President's direction cable to Ambassador Wallace, transmitting substance my letter and instructing Wallace to see French and British authorities and say President agrees with these views and urges compliance. This communication directed to be made orally because of America's position. Lansing read me substance of cable, but for some reason did not feel at liberty to give me copy.[32]

The following letter, dated February 4, 1920, was sent out by Judge Mack, President of the Zionist Organization of America: [33]

The Zionist Organization of America is charged with raising the sum of $10,000,000 in the United States to be expended for the Restoration of Palestine . . .

31. Ibid. (Reel 6)
32. Ibid. (Reel 6)
33. Justice Brandeis was the Honorary President

. . . Many Jews hitherto opposed to the movement have given us assurances of their support and cooperation . . .

. . . Upon our advisory committee are many of the leading men in the country including Secretary Baker, Secretary Daniels, Secretary Lane, Cardinal Gibbons, Former President Eliot of Harvard University, Bishop Burch of New York, the former Ambassador Elkus, Senator Capper, Governor Smith of New York, Hon. William Jennings Bryan and Mr. Jacob H. Schiff . . .

. . . The National Executive Committee has instructed its officers to take immediate steps toward the organization of the campaign for the raising of this sum.[34]

Brandeis re Balfour's cable: The following is a telegram from Brandeis to Mack, dated February 11, 1920:

Balfour cables: Quote: Entirely agree with you that in the interests of Zionism Sykes-Picot Agreement about Northern Frontiers should be modified. As you are aware difficulty is not in London. Suggest your using all your influence elsewhere to the utmost of your power. Unquote.[35]

Cable

To Brandeis from Weizmann and Sokolow, London:

February 12, 1920

The Executive Council of the Zionist Organization assembled in London sends warm greetings to you and your colleagues whose absence from the deliberations is very much deplored. We recognize gratefully services rendered by you during striking political success commencing with Balfour Declaration achieved by the Zionist Organ-

34. *De Haas Papers* (Reel 7)
35. Ibid. (Reel 6)

ization during the period due great measure your ever ready cooperation with activity of the American Zionist Delegation Paris. Your own visit to Europe, Palestine gave incalculable help our cause. Jewish people will never forget that the vast economic resources American Jewry were mobilized by the American Zionists under your leadership thrown powerfully into the scale in favor of Jewish Palestine; when the Mandate for Jewish Palestine definitely allocated still greater scope will be gained. Energies resources American Jewry in cooperation with whole world combine work reconstruction Jewish National Homeland.[36]

Cable

To Brandeis from Weizmann, San Remo:

April 15, 1920

In view of the present critical conditions the presence of our best forces are urgently demanded such as Szold, Felix and others. Beseech you send help with utmost celerity proceeding.[37]

Telegram

To Professor F. Frankfurter, Cambridge, Mass., from De Haas and Mack:

April 16, 1920

Extremely urgent that you be in Washington at Justice Brandeis early tomorrow morning. If possible take seven o'clock train tonight.[38]

36. Ibid. (Reel 7)
37. Ibid. (Reel 7)
38. Ibid. (Reel 7)

Royal Hotel, San Remo, April 24, 1920:

". . . Lloyd George asked me to drive with him today from the hotel to the villa where the Supreme Council meets. On the way he asked me whether I would undertake the administration of Palestine.

. . . Weizmann and Sokolow were then in San Remo and with Lloyd George's consent I discussed the matter with them . . .[39]

. . . Back in London, I set about making preparations for my departure when an unexpected hitch occurred. On May 12th Curzon asked me to come to see him at the Foreign Office. He told me that he had had a very disturbing telegram from Allenby in Cairo, who thought that the appointment of a Jew as the first Governor of Palestine would be likely to be the signal for an outbreak of serious disorder, with widespread attacks upon Jewish settlements and individual Jews.

. . . He asked me whether I did not think it might be better for someone else to go to Palestine for a year to relieve me "of the brunt of the difficulties." [40]

. . . The date fixed for my taking over was July 1st. As the territory was under mandate and not a colony, my designation would be High Commissioner and not Governor.[41]

The departure of Samuel to Palestine as its High Commissioner was the result of the San Remo Conference which opened on April 18, 1920 and on April 25th, the Supreme Council agreed upon the terms of the articles relating to the Mandate to be inserted in the Turkish Treaty. The Balfour Declaration was incorporated in the Peace Treaty with Turkey and Great Britain accepted the Mandate for Palestine.

39. *Grooves of Change, A Book of Memoirs,* Rt. Hon. Viscount Samuel (p. 184)
40. Ibid. (p. 185)
41. Ibid. (p. 186)

Chapter 10

BRANDEIS AFTER SAN REMO: HIS BREACH WITH WEIZMANN ON QUESTIONS OF PRINCIPLE AND METHODS OF ADMINISTRATION

In a letter to the President, dated June 5, 1920, Brandeis writes:

My dear Mr. President:
Our court adjourns Monday and later in the week I sail for England to attend an International Jewish Conference. Through your help and sanction the Balfour Declaration was proclaimed. Through your persisting support it was written into the public laws of the world. You know the longing with which for two thousand years Jews have looked to the fulfillment of the hope of a new Zion, and how the longing has been intensified by recent sufferings. The Jewish people will, I hope, justify your faith and live their gratitude by developing a new Jewish civilization in Palestine, expressed by an example of social justice.[1]

In a letter to the Rt. Hon. Arthur James Balfour, dated June 6, 1920, Brandeis writes:

My dear Mr. Balfour:
In giving to the Jews this opportunity, San Remo has written into the public Law of Nations your faith in the Jewish people and the statesman's courage in acting upon it.

1. *De Haas Papers* (Reel 6)

122

The problems before us are difficult. The burdens are heavy but Jewish spirit, enterprise and self-sacrifice will not be lacking to indicate your faith. The Jewish people will, I believe, develop anew in Palestine a worthy contribution to civilization and to the ever deepening friendship for Britain, live in peaceful neighborliness with other peoples.

Our Court adjourns next week, then I sail to attend an International Jewish Conference in London, and I shall hope that while there I may have the great pleasure of seeing you again.[2]

About three weeks before the World Zionist Conference gathered in London, Weizmann received a confidential letter from Herbert Samuel about the urgent need for financial help.

"As you are aware (Samuel writes) it will be necessary for the Palestine Administration to contract a loan for the purposes of development. A preliminary estimate indicates that a sum of about two million pounds will be needed for the railways, and a further sum of three hundred thousand pounds for public works . . .

. . . In conversation with the Prime Minister on this subject, he expressed the strong view that money for this purpose should be provided from Jewish resources. In view of the most friendly and helpful attitude which has been adopted by the British Government throughout, and of the fact that Palestine is becoming the Jewish National Home, you will, I know, agree that it is a reasonable request. It is very inadvisable that the administration for Palestine should have recourse to the British tax payer for financial assistance.

. . . I should be grateful, therefore, if when Mr. Brandeis and his colleagues are in London, you would discuss the matter with them.[3]

2. Ibid. (Reel 6)
3. Ibid. (Reel 6)

123

The plan which the European leaders had devised for raising money was the establishment of the "Keren Hayesod" (the world-wide fund-raising agency for the support of Zionist activities). Samuel evidently looked forward to a more secure plan.

The World Zionist Conference opened in London, July 7, 1920. It was the first world Zionist gathering in seven years. A large American delegation attended.

"... As soon as Brandeis landed Weizmann hastened to confer with him, plead with him to raise money. Money must be found for reconstruction. With Lord Chief Justice Reading, Brandeis evolved a financial and economic plan to give three year control to a committee of distinguished British Jews, some not previously connected with Zionism. Weizmann kissed his hand and assented.

Brandeis presided at the Conference and declared: "We have come to the time when there are no politics that are valuable except the politics of action." He outlined his reorganization plan. That night, when Brandeis was asleep, Weizmann arranged a meeting with some of the principals and presented a substitute scheme. Brandeis felt betrayed. To his associates he said: "Lloyd George might lie but not to his Cabinet." [4]

While returning to the United States on August 24, 1920, Brandeis drafted on board the *S.S. Zeeland*, a memorandum of the policy he believed the Zionist Organization should adopt. It became known as the "Zeeland Memorandum."

In that memorandum he again elaborated the details of the policy he believed the Zionist Organization should adopt. He stressed the differences between him and his opponents on problems of principle and matters of administration.

... How then shall the money be raised for these general fundamental public utilities? It cannot be left wholly or largely to private enterprise, i.e., investment in the ordi-

4. *Brandeis, The Personal History of an American Ideal,* Alfred Lief (p. 410)

nary sense of the term—because the capitalist would not, with other investment opportunities at hand, incur the risk without the prospect of corresponding profit, and this, in view of the present money conditions and cost of installation, does not exist at all or if it exists, could be effected only through exploitation contrary to the Pittsburgh Program . . .[5]

. . . No part of the money contributed by way of investment or gift should be used in defraying the expenses incurred in raising the money unless the part so to be used shall be clearly set forth in the prospectus in advance of any collection and there must at all times be full and frequent accounting . . .[6]

. . . Furthermore, we must never lose sight of the fact that our plans should be such as to elicit the full cooperation of all the Jews, those who do not want to build up the Zionist Organization but who do want to share with the Zionist Organization in the upbuilding of Palestine.[7]

Reporting about the London Conference to the National Executive Committee in New York on August 29, 1920, immediately upon his return from Europe, explaining his fight for proper methods of management, Brandeis related the following: ". . . It was discovered that the expense of the delegates from the Continent and Palestine, in attendance at the Conference, aggregating 8,000 pounds, had been paid by the London Office. It was also discovered that between last fall and about the time of the Conference, there had been in Palestine an unauthorized expenditure of over 50,000 pounds which had been improperly taken from amounts transmitted by the American organization for specific purposes and institutions. The pressing business of the weeks after the Conference was to devise means for securing repayment of at least part of these misappropriated funds . . ." [8]

The American Zionists were split. The opposition to Brandeis

5. *Louis D. Brandeis, A Biographical Sketch,* Jacob De Haas—"The Zeeland Memorandum" (p. 262-63)
6. Ibid. (p. 271)
7. Ibid. (p. 272)
8. Ibid. "Reorganization Plan" (p. 240)

set to work to oust his regime, and abetted by Weizmann they looked forward to his arrival in the United States.

Greetings to Dr. Chaim Weizmann, President of the World Zionist Organization, by Louis Lipsky, Secretary for Organization.
"Fellow Zionists:
Dr. Chaim Weizmann, President of the World Zionist Organization, is expected to arrive in New York on Sunday, April 3rd.
Dr. Weizmann comes to us with a record of achievement unparalleled in Zionist history. While he was the head of the World Zionist Organization, the Balfour Declaration was issued, the San Remo decision was published, Sr. Herbert Samuel became High Commissioner of Palestine . . .
. . . Dr. Weizmann was at the helm during a period of stress and struggle. Our cause met with opposition from within Jewry and from without. Eastern Europe, formerly the backbone of the Zionist movement, found itself crippled financially and ruined economically. But through all these difficulties Dr. Weizmann led the movement to the realization of our hopes, and the beginning of the practical work of building . . .[9]

This shower of praise for Weizmann recalls a remark by Brandeis in his letter to Weizmann, dated May 22, 1920: ". . . I am happy to know that the Americans have been of service." [10]
The President of the World Zionist Organization arrived in New York on April 3rd and was received all over with tremendous enthusiasm. Five thousand Jews cheered him and the other members of the Zionist Delegation at the Metropolitan Opera House.

Judge Mack about his Negotiations with Weizmann

In a letter to Weizmann, dated April 24, 1921, Mack writes:

9. *The New Palestine*, March 18, 1921
10. *De Hass Papers* (Reel 6)

I acknowledge receipt of your letter dated April 20th. Following the adoption of the resolution of the Executive Committee of the Zionist Organization of America on April 10th, you and I had a number of conferences. We reached certain conclusions. On Saturday night, April 16th, you definitely agreed that the "Keren Hayesod" in the United States should be exclusively a donation fund.

During the night, four secretaries all selected by you including even the one acting for me, formulated a draft for the agreement. On April 17th this was submitted to each of us. While my associates and I were considering the document, you personally telephoned that you rejected the draft, and that you would issue your proclamation at once.

. . . As I reiterated to you in the whole course of our conference, the creation in America of a donation fund separate from investments, in accordance with the unanimous decision of the Zionist Organization of America, and the proper and adequate safeguarding of the expenditure in Palestine of all sums collected, are prerequisites from which it is impossible for the Zionist Organization to depart; these are the real issues involved. They are fundamental in our conception of the standards of trusteeship which we must at all hazards observe.

. . . While it was agreed in London last summer, that a Board of Trustees would be established and a detailed monthly report of all receipts and expenditures would be ordered, so far as we are aware, no practical steps have been taken to put these proposals into effect. Moreover, the financial control established in Palestine by the Reorganization Commission through a responsible treasurer, is in danger of being overthrown by some of your associates . . .[11]

The Cleveland Convention

The 24th Annual Convention of the Zionist Organization of America opened on Sunday, June 5, 1921.

11. *The New Palestine,* May 16, 1921

. . . In the course of his address, Dr. Wise hinted that though the present leaders may not be retained in office, they will remain in the movement and work loyally as mere soldiers in the ranks . . .

. . . Frankfurter in his speech indicted the European leadership for allowing itself to be controlled by a group of men who are at the head of the "Keren Hayesod."

. . . It was a tense and dramatic moment when the roll was called.

. . . And the vote was announced: 153 against a vote of confidence, 71 for.

. . . Judge Mack expressed his gratitude to the American Zionists for having chosen him President of the organization for three years in succession, at the most critical time in the development of Zionism, for having given him the opportunity to take part in the work of meeting the great problems that had confronted and still were confronting Zionism.

. . . Judge Mack then read the following letter of resignation from Justice Louis D. Brandeis, Honorary President of the Zionist Organization of America:

"My dear Judge Mack:

With the principles and policies adopted by the National Executive Committee under your leadership I am in complete agreement. Strict adherence to these principles is demanded by the high Zionist ideals. Steadfast pursuit of these policies is essential to early and worthy development of Palestine and the Jewish Homeland. We who believe in these principles and policies can not properly take part in any administration of Zionist affairs which repudiates them.

Upon the delegates in convention assembled rests the responsibility of deciding whether these principles and policies shall prevail in the immediate future. If their decision is adverse, you will, I assume, resign, and in that event present also my resignation as Honorary President. Our place will then be as humble soldiers in the ranks to hasten by our struggle the coming of the day when principles and

128

policies in which we believe will be recognized as the only ones through which our great ends may be achieved." [12]

Even after 1921 Justice Brandeis was influential in broader fields of organization to translate the Zionist ideals into reality. After the Cleveland Convention Brandeis and his followers met in New York and pledged themselves to undertake immediate constructive work in Palestine without seceding from the Zionist Organization or forming a minority group within the movement. Brandeis continued uninterruptedly his work for the economic rebirth of Palestine. He was, for instance, one of the founders of the Palestine Cooperative Company, the predecessor of the Palestine Economic Corporation which has been playing a very important role in the economic and industrial development of Palestine and now Israel. He sponsored the incorporation in 1922, of the Palestine Endowment Funds, Inc., of which Judge Mack was the first President, for educational and charitable purposes.

It is beyond the scope of this book to enter into a detailed description of Brandeis' Zionist activities after his resignation.

The following story told by David Ben Gurion, former Prime Minister of Israel, will illustrate how Brandeis, as a "humble soldier in the ranks" translated into action his duties toward the Jewish Homeland.

". . . This was in the year 1933, when I was for the first time elected to the Zionist leadership and I decided to go to one man whom I knew and respected, to the American Supreme Court Justice Brandeis, in the belief that he will understand the importance of the matter. I presented to him a memorandum about the importance of the "Negev" and the future of "Eilat," which can unite us with the Asiatic Continent. I emphasized in the memorandum that in spite of the existence of the Suez Canal it is quite uncertain that England will remain there forever. The canal is not a safe road to Asia because one sunken ship can block this road. There is, however, an open road to Asia through the Red Sea. It is for this reason that it is

12. *The New Palestine*, June 17, 1921

important to establish on that spot a "Haluzim (Pioneers) Jewish Settlement" which will not bring any profits and this project will probably cost one hundred thousand dollars.

I had barely finished my last sentence when Brandeis told me: here are your hundred thousand dollars.

I told him that I did not come to ask him for money. I only came to ask his moral support for this work. However, Brandeis told me: "I want to have the privilege to be the first one to help lay the foundation on that spot." [13]

Thinking that there might have been a mistake in the figures, the author wrote to Ben Gurion asking him whether the donation amounted to ten or to one hundred thousand dollars. In a letter dated July 4, 1965, Ben Gurion replied: "It was not ten thousand dollars but one hundred thousand dollars that Brandeis gave me for the establishment of a settlement at the port of the Red Sea."

13. *Memoirs*, David Ben Gurion. *The Day—Jewish Journal*, June 5, 1964